THE SEDUCTION OF THE EPISCOPAL CHURCH

THE SEDUCTION OF THE EPISCOPAL CHURCH

J2B Publishing LLC
4251 Columbia Park Road
Pomfret, MD 20675
www.J2BLLC.com

This book is set in Garamond

Cover artwork by Mary Barrows

ISBN: 978-1-948747-49-3

THE SEDUCTION OF THE EPISCOPAL CHURCH

DAVID W. VIRTUE

COMMENDATIONS

David Virtue's widely educated and globally traveled experience should not be missed. He is unashamed of the Gospel and he continues to deliver spirited critiques of church leaders who are substituting the teachings of secular society for the Christian faith. The Episcopal Church has moved, over the years, from its official magazines, The Spirit of Mission to Forward then to The Episcopalian, and now to nothing. His reporting is thus especially needed to light up the present darkness of Episcopal and Anglican events. Some will always disagree with David, but he remains accessible to correction and indefatigably committed to the Christian faith.

—Bishop C. FitzSimons Allison (Diocese of South Carolina, ret.)

I have been given the privilege of reading the material prepared by David Virtue for his book, and am impressed by his in-depth documentation of the many actions taken by the leadership of The Episcopal Church to subvert the clear teaching of the Christian Faith, and to drive out all who would defend and proclaim that Faith. A sad but true tale.

—Bishop William Wantland (Diocese of Eau Claire, ret.)

David Virtue has been a clear and not always uncontroversial voice for biblical orthodoxy within the Episcopal Church USA. This book gives his perspective in a lively style and it will be a great help to those who wish to understand the decline and division that liberalism has inflicted on the church. As someone who experienced 6 years as a member of the House of Bishops (2002-2008) I was glad to be received back into the Church of England when the Presiding Bishop 'received the renunciation of my orders'.

—Bishop Henry Scriven, English Anglican bishop

In his new book David Virtue traces the contemporary history and state of The Episcopal Church as seen through the eyes of its bishops and presiding bishops. From Bishop James Pike to Presiding Bishop Michael Curry, the author traces the decline of the Church as it increasingly abandons Scripture and embraces the world's values, particularly in the area of pansexuality, resulting in a mass hemorrhaging of Episcopalians leading to the formation of the Anglican Church in North America. This volume is a wakeup call to The Episcopal Church and any denomination that abandons God's Word in favor of the zeitgeist. It should be a reminder that when a Church sows to the wind it reaps the whirlwind.

—The Most Rev. Gregory Venables, Archbishop of South America

David Virtue gives us, as always, a swashbuckling account of the demise of a once significant denomination which sought to be a via media between Protestants and Catholics. We don't have to agree with every word of his to realize that, as ever, it was the leadership that has let down the faithful. His account should drive us to our knees for true shepherds who will, under God, lead the flock to green pastures and still waters, not into the deserts of syncretism and the following of every fad on offer in a decadent West.

—The Rt. Rev. Michael Nazir-Ali (Rochester, UK, ret.)

CONTENTS

The Seduction of the Episcopal Church

FOREWORD

A crisis of authority has gripped and is destroying a once proud American denomination

There is a rottenness in the Church that must be addressed, writes author and social critic Dr. Os Guinness. In this book I have attempted to address precisely that. The Episcopal Church has lost its theological moorings and has ventured out into waters that no denomination has ever gone before, with catastrophic results and profound spiritual consequences.

This is the story of a once proud Christian denomination that stood as a landmark church in a nation that has seen presidents, senators and business leaders pass through its hallowed red doors.

Today those doors are fast closing as churches empty, dioceses juncture and priests, parishes and parishioners flee to safer spiritual climes.

For more than forty years Episcopalians have been drinking from the poisoned chalice of pansexuality and the taste has been both bitter and deadly. Spiritual and ecclesiastical death marks the present and future state of this denomination.

As homosexual acceptance swept through the Church, orthodox priests were strangled with the cinctures of revisionist bishops happy to immolate them on the altar of their pansexual God.

Convinced homosexuals have only ever been a small minority in the Episcopal Church, but their cries for acceptance and their relentless drive rattled the hierarchy and forced a crisis that changed the Episcopal Church forever, pushing it in a deadly direction from which it has never recovered. To paraphrase Jaroslav Pelikan, Episcopalians have become the dead faith of the living.

Numbers Don't Lie

In 2013 TEC membership stood at 1,838,563, by 2017 it had dropped to 1,705,254. In 2018 that figure had dropped to 1,676,349. Average Sunday attendance for the same period went from 611,686 to 553,927. By 2018 the Church had shed another 23,538 in Sunday attendance.

The Episcopal Church Annual, also known as The Red Book, finds the high point of Episcopal membership in 1966 at 3,647,297. By 2002 the total number of members had plunged to 2,320,221. The Episcopal Church has lost well over a million members during the last 35 years.

Some 90% of Episcopalians are white, while some 62.1% of all Americans are white. 31% of Episcopalians are 65 or older. 79% of Episcopalians do not have a child under 18. 58 is now the median average Sunday attendance (ASA). 71% of Episcopal congregations have an ASA of 100 or fewer. 4% of Episcopal congregations have an ASA of 300 or more. 55% of Episcopal congregations have lost 10 percent in ASA (past 5 years).

In August of 2015, a survey, commissioned by VIRTUEONLINE, conducted by Joshua de Gastyne - an independent survey group - and funded by an outside donor, revealed that women disproportionately attend Episcopal churches by almost two to one over men and children.

651 surveys were collected from 7,128 Episcopal churches in the United States, giving 95% confidence that cohort answers are representative with a 3.7% margin of error.

Some 32% of all parishes are served by women priests with the average attendance of women slightly more than 62%. The remaining 38% were mostly men with a sprinkling of children.

More telling statistics reveal that 45% of all Episcopal parishes in the Episcopal Church no longer have a full-time paid priest or only a part-time non-stipendiary priest officiating. That's almost one in two parishes with no discernible Episcopal leadership.

Episcopalians' Beliefs, Values & Biblical Literacy

As an indicator of how spiritually sick The Episcopal Church has become, the latest figures reveal that 47% of Episcopalians say the Bible is not the Word of God and 51% of Episcopalians seldom or never read Scripture. Only 18% of Episcopalians primarily look to religion for guidance on right and wrong while 79% of Episcopalians think abortion should be legal in all or most cases. Some 74% of Episcopalians favor same-sex marriage.

Only about one third of all Episcopalians practice their faith. A typical example would be the Diocese of Long Island which claims some 43,440 Episcopalians. Only 13,000 of them go to church on an average Sunday. Long Island is the home of 7.8 million people which means that only 0.55% of Long Islanders are Episcopalians. This includes Brooklyn and Queens.

The National Church (1965 & 2015)

In 1965 some 3.62 million Americans claimed to be Episcopalians. Over 194 million people lived in the United States then. 1.9% of Americans were Episcopalians in that year.

By 2015, 1.91 million people were Episcopalians. Some 579,780 of them went to church on an average Sunday. America's population was by then 321.4 million people. Of that number just 0.55% of Americans were Episcopalians.

In 1965 some 880,000 children were enrolled in Episcopal Church schools. By 2014 only 188,418 children are enrolled in Episcopal Church schools, a 78.6% decline in. By 2017 churchwide enrollment was 161,000. This is a drop of 81.7% or 719,000 students from 1965 to 2017!

In 1965 128,000 people were confirmed in the Episcopal Church, in 2014, 21,317 people were confirmed in the Episcopal Church, a decline of 83.3% decline in Episcopal confirmations. By 2018 some 19,142 (7,942 children; 9,500 adults) were confirmed in the entire Episcopal Church a drop of 118,858 or a decline of 85%.

Since then the decline in all attendance has only accelerated. With the consecration of an avowed homosexual to the episcopacy in 2003, the Episcopal Church went on to experience the worst single outflow of Episcopalians in modern history. More than 100,000 Episcopalians left the Episcopal Church. The church has never recovered.

ACKNOWLEDGMENTS

I want to thank my faithful copy-editor Diane Amison-Loring for her indefatigable efforts to read and edit this book. Her unerring instinct for repetition and grammar, and her ability to improve the text, I cannot thank enough. To my friend and attorney, John H. Lewis Jr., who read the text and kept me from going over the top, I am eternally grateful. To Mary Ann Mueller, VOL's special correspondent and research assistant who worked tirelessly to make sure the facts were accurate and kept me from going astray, I will always be in her debt.

David W. Virtue, DD

VIRTUEONLINE

INTRODUCTION

For the time is coming when people will not endure sound teaching, but having itching ears they will accumulate for themselves teachers to suit their own passions. (2 Tim 4:3).

On Nov. 3, 2003 in Durham, New Hampshire some 2,500 Episcopalians including 53 ECUSA bishops and a handful of guests, marched into the Whittemore Center at the University of New Hampshire. They proceeded to lay hands on Gene Robinson, an actively homosexual priest and made him Bishop Coadjutor. On March 7, 2004, he would become the bishop ordinary.

It was a defining moment not only for V. Gene Robinson, who embraced his lover, Mark Andrews, his ex-wife and his two daughters, it was an ecclesiastical tsunami wave that not only swept over the Episcopal Church that night, but in time would sweep over the entire Anglican Communion.

The Presider and Chief Consecrator was Frank Griswold. One of the co-consecrators was former Presiding Bishop Edmond Browning.

I sat in the bleachers watching and listening. Three persons protested; one was a priest, the Rev. Dr. Earle Fox, another was a lay woman, Meredith Harwood from St. Mark's Episcopal Church in Ashland, NH. In an emotional plea, Harwood cried out, "Inclusivity without transformation is not the gospel of Jesus Christ. It will break God's heart."

The third protester was Bishop David Bena, the Suffragan Bishop of Albany. He stood up and read a statement on behalf of 38 ECUSA and Canadian bishops and said the chosen lifestyle of Robinson was incompatible with Scripture and that to proceed with this consecration "stands at odds with that teaching."

It was all to no avail. The fix was in, the die had been cast, 62 Bishops of The Episcopal Church had given Robinson their consents to his ordination and consecration to be a bishop in the Church of God, the 993rd bishop in church succession. The face of North American Anglicanism had changed forever.

Outgoing New Hampshire Bishop Douglas Theuner stood up and said, "You will stand as a symbol of unity as no one else ever has... I believe the episcopate is more a symbol of unity now than it ever has been." Theuner slammed unnamed persons whom he called "detractors" because they saw in this a "divine battle in the war for the Anglican soul." It isn't, he said.

He was wrong. It was, in fact, the turning point for faithful Episcopalians and Anglicans across North America. What had begun in 1999 with the fledgling Anglican Mission in America (AMiA), would morph and expand over time and become the Anglican Church in North America (ACNA).

Following the Robinson consecration, Evangelical and Anglo-Catholic Episcopalians began the long march out of the Episcopal Church. Faithful priests faced deposition, loss of parishes and, in some cases, loss of pensions. Lives were torn apart, but the majority of the House of Bishops stood firm under pressure from Church attorneys and watched as more than 100,000 faithful Episcopalians, more than 700 hundred priests and more than a dozen bishops were evicted from the Episcopal Church.

A cry went up. Who will save us? Orthodox Global South provinces came to the rescue and gave ecclesiastical cover to those who fled. In June of 2008, the Global Anglican Futures Conference (GAFCON) was born to address the growing controversies and divisions in the Anglican Communion. GAFCON drew together African, Asian and Latin American provinces and dioceses in North America to form a new holy alliance.

The first GAFCON gathering took place in Jerusalem with Anglican leaders representing a clear majority of the world's practicing Anglicans. They produced and joyously affirmed the Global Anglican Future

Conference (GAFCON) Statement and the Jerusalem Declaration at the end of the conference on Sunday June 29, 2008. It signaled a new reality for the Anglican Communion.

The document addressed the crisis gripping the Anglican Communion over scriptural authority. It called for the creation of a new council of primates overseeing a volunteer fellowship committed to mission and biblical Anglicanism as well as a new structure of accountability based on the Jerusalem Declaration. It also signaled the move of most of the world's practicing Anglicans into a post-colonial reality, where the Archbishop of Canterbury is recognized for his historic role, but not as the only arbiter of what it means to be Anglican.

A primates' council was formed by the six Anglican primates from Kenya, Nigeria, Rwanda, Southern Cone, Uganda and West Africa.

The Primates' Council was tasked with recognizing and authenticating "confessing Anglican jurisdictions, clergy and congregations and to encourage all Anglicans to promote the gospel and defend the faith." From the outset, the statement recognized the "desirability of territorial jurisdiction for provinces and dioceses of the Anglican Communion except in areas where churches and leaders have denied the orthodox faith or are preventing its spread."

The GAFCON Primates believed that the "time is now ripe for the formation of a province in North America for the federation currently known as Common Cause Partnership to be recognized by the Primates' Council." The statement described those participating in this new movement as "A fellowship of Confessing Anglicans." It asserted the intention of all those involved to remain Anglican.

"Our fellowship is not breaking away from the Anglican Communion. We, together with many other faithful Anglicans throughout the world, believe the doctrinal foundation of Anglicanism, which defines our core identity as Anglicans, is expressed in these words: The doctrine of the Church is grounded in the Holy Scriptures and in such teachings of the ancient Fathers and Councils of the Church as are agreeable to the said Scriptures. In particular, such doctrine is to be found in the Thirty-nine Articles of Religion, the Book of Common Prayer and the Ordinal."

The GAFCON Primates took a dramatic step when they declared that worldwide Anglicanism had now entered a post-colonial phase. Instead of continuing to rely solely on the colonial structures that had served the Anglican Communion so poorly during the present crisis, the movement now was to accept all those Anglicans who affirmed the Anglican standard of faith. "While acknowledging the nature of Canterbury as an historic see, we do not accept that Anglican identity is determined necessarily through recognition by the Archbishop of Canterbury," they wrote. This conference and what flowed from it was a sea change.

The GAFCON Statement concluded by saying that the Anglican Communion should and will be reformed around the biblical gospel and mandate to go into all the world and present Christ to the nations.

The Jerusalem Declaration was produced at GAFCON with the participation of all 1148 delegates, representing more than 35 million practicing Anglicans worldwide. A new day had dawned.

This book is written to help Episcopalians in North America and Anglicans worldwide, especially those in the Global South understand what has been going on for the last 40 years in The Episcopal Church North America.

The picture is not a pretty one. In the words of the hymn writer, "Though with a scornful wonder, men see her sore oppressed, by schisms rent asunder, by heresies distressed," the Episcopal Church has, by its actions, torn the fabric of the Anglican Communion through its embrace of pansexuality, denied the Creed and abandoned the authority of Scripture. In some cases, the Episcopal Church has violated the consciences of priests who could not accept the ordination of women to the priesthood, even to the point of syncretism with other religions.

What will emerge in these pages is the picture of a Church that was once faithful to the gospel, tradition, history and Scripture, but over the past four decades revolted against Scripture and become intoxicated with the spirit of the age.

Even as this is being written, the same trajectory of this struggle is beginning to play out in the Church of England. Homosexual acceptance nibbles away at Church doctrine and teaching along with the ordination of women to the episcopacy, unacceptable to both Evangelicals and Anglo-Catholics.

The response of the orthodox in America resulted in large numbers of Anglicans deciding that they could no longer belong to a Church that had reconfigured the Apostolic and Biblical DNA. In 2009, they left. The ACNA was born. This new branch of Anglicanism now has 30 missionary dioceses, over 1,000 congregations and more than 135,000 members.

You will wonder, be amazed and shocked at how a single denomination that traces its roots back some 400 years could stray so far from the faith once entrusted to it. But stray she did and today the Episcopal Church has seen staggering losses in parishioners of more than 1.5 million, while Episcopal clergy numbers have increased by 62% from 9,079 to 14,694, even as the institution sharply declined and the bureaucratic structure grew.

Four presiding bishops have been the culprits in the Episcopal Church's decline, and their lives and ministries are documented in this book. They have swung the Episcopal Church in a direction that few believe she can ever recover from.

David W. Virtue, DD

VIRTUEONLINE

www.virtueonline.org

BISHOP JAMES PIKE

His Tragic Life, Death, and Heresies

James Albert Pike might be thought of as the Episcopal Church's first public heretic.

Born on St. Valentine's Day in Oklahoma City on February 14, 1913, Pike's father died when he was two, and his mother, an indomitable figure, married California attorney Claude McFadden. The young Pike was a Roman Catholic and considered the priesthood; however, while attending the University of Santa Clara he came to consider himself an agnostic.

Pike obtained his undergraduate degree from the University of Southern California, later obtaining law degrees from Yale Law School. After leaving Yale, he served as a staff attorney for the Securities and Exchange Commission in Washington, DC, during Franklin D. Roosevelt's New Deal Era and then taught law as a lecturer at the Catholic University of America and George Washington University. During the Second World War, he served with Naval Intelligence.

Though he was originally from Oklahoma, Pike was never comfortable with the values of America's heartland. He lived most of his adult life in the urban centers of the East and West and, because of it, was clearly out of touch with the average Episcopalian.

Pike's personal life was as messy as his later theological ramblings.

Pike's first marriage to Jane Alvies was annulled in 1941. He married Esther Yanovsky in 1942; she filed for divorce from Pike in 1965 (finalized in 1966). They had four children, two boys and two girls. In 1968, he married Diane Kennedy (born 1938). She was almost half his age. He was 56 and she was 31. Diane Kennedy Pike was the executive director of a foundation which conducted research into life after death.

After the Second World War, Pike and his second wife joined the Episcopal Church. Pike studied and decided that he had a vocation. Since he had already been married twice, his first brief (one-year) marriage had to be annulled, and there were suggestions at the time that this was accomplished by subterfuge and incomplete disclosure.

He first entered Virginia Theological Seminary (1945–1946) and then Union Theological Seminary (Bachelor of Divinity, 1951) to prepare for the priesthood. He was ordained in 1946, first serving as an assistant at St. John's Episcopal Church, Lafayette Square in Washington, DC, before accepting a joint appointment as Rector of Christ Church and Episcopal chaplain at Vassar College in Poughkeepsie, New York. In 1949, he became head of the department of religion and chaplain at Columbia University.

Remaining on the adjunct faculty of Columbia, Pike became the Dean of the Cathedral of St. John the Divine in 1952. He got the highly sought-after position thanks to influential friends in high Episcopal circles, particularly two bishops, Charles Gilbert and Horace W.B. Donegan. Using his new position and media savvy, he vociferously opposed the local Catholic bishops over their attacks on Planned Parenthood and their opposition to birth control. He accepted an invitation to receive an honorary doctorate from the University of the South in Tennessee, but then publicly declined after finding that the university did not admit African Americans. "It is clear that the present faculty stand is 'on the side of the angels' and I feel I must stand with them," he said in a letter to the trustees.

An example of Pike's use of the media is how he released his letter to *The New York Times* before it was delivered to Sewanee's trustees: they heard the news when reporters called for reactions. It was also at this time that he publicly challenged Senator Joseph McCarthy's allegation that 7,000 American pastors were part of a Kremlin conspiracy; when the newly elected President Dwight D. Eisenhower backed up Pike, McCarthy and his movement began to lose their influence.

In New York, Pike reached a large audience with liberal sermons and weekly television programs. Common topics included birth control, abortion laws, racism, capital punishment, apartheid, antisemitism and farm worker exploitation.

Pike continued to serve as curate at a church in Washington, DC, commuting regularly to New York to take classes at Union Theological Seminary, presided over then by Reinhold Niebuhr an American Reformed theologian, ethicist, commentator on politics and public affairs.

Pike first came to public attention for his belligerent rhetoric — from the pulpit and outside it — on the right. In 1947, just as the House Committee on Un-American Activities was getting underway, Pike captured headlines by denouncing the faculty of Vassar College as "Unitarian, humanist, materialist, and Marxist"; his evidence was little more than one Vassar girl's essay questioning the Virgin Birth (a doctrine the radicalized Pike of the 1960s would repudiate with great fanfare). Then he called on Christian churches to purge Communists in their midst and do battle against "secular humanists."

Among other initiatives, Pike launched a weekly television show on ABC called Dean Pike, which soon eclipsed Bishop Fulton J. Sheen's long-running Life Is Worth Living. The program made celebrities of Pike and his wife, Esther. They offered harmless chitchat about a topic, with Pike weighing in at the end to give what he called "a five-minute commercial for God." Between 1952 and 1958 he also wrote twelve books, including quite orthodox and widely read titles like *Doing the Truth and Beyond Anxiety*. By 1966, his fame brought him a TIME magazine cover.

Election as bishop

Pike was elected bishop coadjutor of California in 1958 and succeeded to the See a few months later, following the death of his predecessor, Karl Morgan Block. He served in this position until 1966, when he resigned to become a senior fellow for the Center for the Study of Democratic Institutions in Santa Barbara, California, a liberal think tank founded by Robert Maynard Hutchins. During this period, he was an adjunct professor at the University of California, Berkeley, School of Law (1966–1967) and the Graduate Theological Union (1966). His episcopate was marked by both professional and personal controversy.

He was one of the leaders of the Protestants and Other Americans United for the Separation of Church and State movement, which advocated against John F. Kennedy's presidential campaign because of Catholic teachings.

While at Grace Cathedral, he was involved with promoting a living wage for workers in San Francisco, the acceptance of homosexual people in the church and civil rights. He also recognized a Methodist minister as having dual ordination and freedom to serve in the diocese.

In 1964, the General Convention changed the canons to read that deaconesses were "ordered" rather than "appointed" and adopted a special liturgy for use in the ordination of women as deaconesses. The convention also dropped the celibacy requirement for deaconesses. Furthermore, it declared deaconesses to be an order of the ministry

– adding a fourth order to the Anglican orders of ministry. Pike became involved in the debate because of his desire for women – and particularly a deaconess in his diocese – to be allowed to become deacons.

William Stringfellow, an American lay theologian, lawyer and social activist and Anthony Towne, author, satirist and poet, explained the theologically confusing issue in a fairly succinct manner in their book, *The Death and Life of Bishop Pike.*

A deaconess, Mrs. Phyllis Edwards of San Francisco who distinguished herself with her ministry to the poor in the inner city, caught Pike's attention and he announced his intention of admitting Mrs. Edwards to the diaconate. Pike believed the term "ordered" could refer to nothing other than ordination to the full ministry, just as it did for male ordinands. Over objections from national and local church leaders, Pike deferred a decision until he could bring the issue before the September 1965 House of Bishops meeting in Glacier Park, Montana. Later in September 1965, he ordained Edwards as a first-order deacon, now known as a "transitional deacon", usually the first step in the process towards ordination in the priesthood in the Episcopal church. The ordination, however, was not approved until after Pike's death.

Among his notable accomplishments, Pike invited Martin Luther King Jr. to speak at Grace Cathedral in San Francisco in 1965 following his march to Selma, Alabama.

Pike's Growing Disenchantment with Orthodoxy

Pike's theology fell apart over time involving the rejection of central Christian beliefs. His writings questioned a number of widely accepted beliefs, including the virginity of Mary, the Mother of Jesus, the doctrine of Hell and the Trinity. He famously called for "fewer beliefs, more belief."

On three separate occasions, (1962, 1964, 1965,) a bill of particulars alleging heresy against Pike was presented at Episcopal synods, each bill growing in intensity. On each occasion, the bishops elected to follow the path of compromise and a full-blown heresy trial was averted. It was politics as usual in the Episcopal House of Bishops. In October 1966, he was formally censured by his fellow Bishops. As Bishop C. FitzSimons Allison noted, bishops have a sworn obligation to guard the faith, but this was strikingly absent since Bishop James Pike's denial of the doctrine of Christ and the Trinity. Pike was censured by the House of Bishops for the "tone and manner" but not for the substance of his teaching. This was the same year his son James, Jr. committed suicide.

In December 1960, Pike had an essay published in Look magazine in which he argued that the Church was no longer relevant for contemporary life. (Shades of John Shelby Spong). He became a severe critic of the Church, her Tradition and the Bible.

Never comfortable with Evangelicalism in any of its manifestations, Pike had spoken out, for example, against the practice of glossolalia or speaking in tongues. Any such manifestations of religious enthusiasm he condemned as "inconsistent with the sacramental theology of the Holy Catholic Church." But things were to change.

Pike's dissent from this orthodox-sounding invocation to theological liberalism, then to Gnosticism was slow. Just when he became an outright heretic is difficult to pinpoint.

In 1964, Bishop Pike gave a lecture on eternal life and social action now. "I don't believe in the immortality of the soul, actually, I don't believe in the existence of the soul. I do believe in eternal life and social action right now."

As one commentator pointed out, Pike was an inveterate "trendy," not wishing ever "to be even slightly behind the curve of a coming spiritual movement." On the other hand, he often sounded orthodox; indeed, his last and fatal trip to Israel was undertaken so that he could walk where Jesus had walked.

Pike's incessant womanizing and drinking caused ripples of concern in the church; still, in 1958 he was popular enough to be narrowly (by one vote) nominated to become Bishop of California (meaning the San Francisco area).

By this time, he had publicly dispensed with the Virgin Birth, the Trinity, salvation by grace and the uniqueness of God's revelation in Jesus Christ. (Today this may sound unexceptional, but back then such heresies were not commonplace.)

He won the election, but the process was divisive. First, his slippery annulment of his first marriage became an issue; then opposition to his increasingly heretical views coalesced.

In San Francisco, Pike proved a good fundraiser and a capable administrator. But his personal life was increasingly out of control; for example, he had a clandestine telephone installed in the bishop's office for the exclusive use of whomever he was having an affair with.

Esther, his wife, filed for divorce in 1965. A year later, his eldest son, Jim, committed suicide at age 20. A year after that, his secretary/mistress, Maren Bergrud, killed herself in his apartment with an overdose of sleeping pills. He dragged her comatose body down the hall to her own apartment, lied to the police and destroyed evidence, but was sufficiently composed to conduct her funeral service a few days later.

Pike met the Christian apologist Elton Trueblood at a conference in Alaska; there was correspondence between the men in 1955. Trueblood taught Philosophy at Earlham College and mentions Pike's apostacy in his book *The Company of the Committed.*

Pike's last sad years were consumed by spiritualism. Through several "mediums," he attempted to communicate with his dead son and eventually persuaded himself that he had done so. By this time, he had become an embarrassment, and when in 1968 he offered his resignation as Bishop of California, it was received with alacrity.

In April 1969, Pike made life even easier for his church by formally announcing he was leaving, calling the Episcopal Church (in a *Look magazine* article) "a sick—even dying—institution." In this, at least, the bishop may be said to have been prophetic.

The year 1977 was a critical year for the United States and for the Episcopal Church, writes David E. Sumner in his book *The Episcopal*

Church's History 1945-1985. The church's membership showed a slight increase, but it was to be the last increase for fifteen years. Baptisms took the biggest dip since 1962. The "Doctrine Debaters," Bishop James Pike in the US and Bishop John A. T. Robinson in England were challenging the basic tenets of the Christian faith, while Thomas J. J. Altizer and William Hamilton were proclaiming "the death of God."

Pike's Demise

It was August 1969, the year of the moon landing. Bishop James Pike and Diane, his third wife, went to Israel to gather material for a book Pike was writing. The book was to present Pike's version of the origins of Christianity. On September 2nd they set out in a rented car for the wilderness where Jesus was tempted by the devil.

After passing Herodion, Pike turned off on an unpaved track which he believed led north to Jericho. In fact, he was at the beginning of Wadi Mashash, leading east towards the Dead Sea. Soon the unpaved road ended where it had been washed out by flash floods. The Pikes tried to turn around, but the rear wheels of the car dropped into a deep rut. They couldn't free the car and didn't know how to use the jack.

The Pikes abandoned the car after trying unsuccessfully to get it out of the rut. Then they walked for two hours until Bishop Pike was too exhausted to go on. They found a relatively flat rock under a bit of an overhang that gave them some shade. As the sun was setting, Diane Pike left her husband and continued walking. After some ten hours of climbing steep canyons in the moonlight, she stumbled onto the road being built between Ein Gedi and Ein Fashha. A security guard found her and she was taken to police authorities in Bethlehem.

When they returned to the place where Diane had left her husband, they found the map that Diane had left with her husband, but no clue as to where he had gone.

After three days of temperatures above 100 degrees, the hunt for Bishop Pike was called off. At a news conference, Mrs. Pike reported that the seer who had put her husband in contact with the spirit of his son had had a vision of him alive in a cave near the place Diane had left him. Off duty army scouts and local Bedouin searched for him, but his body was not found.

It took rescue parties five days to find Pike. On September 7th, Pike's body was found. He had been climbing a steep ascent in Wadi Mashash when he slipped and fell to his death. He had apparently fallen from a canyon ridge about sixty feet onto a ledge. Baked in the merciless sun, his body was already in an advanced state of decomposition. Pike was buried in St. Peter's cemetery in Jaffa under a tamarisk tree. Before his death in 1969, Pike had announced that he and Diane were ending their affiliation with the Episcopal Church.

What should we make of Bishop James Pike? Certain saints excepted, perhaps, any man's life is a tangled skein of good and evil, right and wrong, darkness and light; that being so, it is churlish, perhaps uncharitable, to say that nothing so became Bishop Pike's life as his leaving of it.

Pike's Apostacy

In a YouTube interview, Pike mocked Christian doctrine based, he said, on Copernicus's Revolution, which launched modern astronomy and the Scientific Revolution which Pike said did away with a three-tiered universe and much that was literal about the Christian Faith

When asked by a TV interviewer if Christ ascended into heaven, Pike said no, based on his understanding of Copernicus. "I don't believe Jesus sat next to his Father, but Jesus continued in an ongoing life. When asked if he believed in the ascension of Jesus, Pike said he did not. We can't talk about up and down since Copernicus. I don't believe in these physical images."

When asked where eternity would find him, he answered, "living on and on with the hang-ups that I have with various blocks to be worked to encounters. When I die, I will be just the Jim Pike I am now. I have gotten rid of some idols out of my life and those that still remain in freedom, God doesn't arm twist us."

The Tragedy of James Pike

In an essay on Pike, cultural anthropologist Alice C. Linsley asked the question, "Has occult involvement by Anglicans contributed to the spiritual decay of the Episcopal Church?" The answer of course is yes. Pike dabbled deeply in the occult as he sought to get in touch with his son who had committed suicide.

Many bishops have been lax in upholding the doctrine and discipline of the Church and this has turned Anglicanism into a schismatic brand of modernist Christianity. In this tragedy, the Episcopal Church bears a large portion of the shame, beginning at least as early as James Albert Pike.

Pike was the precursor, perhaps even the prognosticator of things to come. It would be downhill for The Episcopal Church from then on. In time, the Episcopal Church would not only fully embrace women to the priesthood, but to the episcopacy and, with the full embrace of pansexuality, the church would draw into its fold openly practicing lesbian and homosexual priests and bishops, with homosexual marriage being the end of the pansexual experiment.

In the ensuing years, tens of thousands of Episcopalians would leave the Church, orthodox priests would be deposed, parishes would be torn from these orthodox priests and whole dioceses would leave. The seduction of the Episcopal Church would now begin in earnest.

SOURCES:

David M. Robertson is the author of *Lost Shepherd A Passionate Pilgrim: A Biography of Bishop James A. Pike.*

Ian Hunter is Emeritus Professor of Intellectual History in the Institute for Advanced Studies in the Humanities at the University of Queensland.

David E. Sumner is the author of *The Episcopal Church's History 1945-1985*

THE SEDUCTIVE WORK OF LOUIE CREW

The Beginning of Integrity

When Dr. Louie Crew taught at Rutgers University in 1989-2001, he tells the story about starting some of his "Bible as Literature" classes. Crew would walk briskly into the class bearing a large bowl of dirty water. He placed the bowl prominently on a table in front of the class and would wait for a moment.

After the suspense built, Crew picked up a copy of the Bible and dropped the book into the muddy water. The class of college students would gasp. After retrieving the soggy, dirty Bible, he displayed this to the class and announced, "See! No lightning bolts!"

Following dousing the Bible in dirty water, Crew would declare his understanding of the scriptures. "The Bible is 66 books and all in various states of understanding of who God is." He taught at the university level what is called in academic circles as the "critical understanding of the Bible." Crew states, "This book is called the Holy Bible. This is not something it gets because someone prints it on the cover."

Crew correctly identified an important issue in the homosexual controversy he believed in and would, in time, push onto the Episcopal Church. Many disagree about what constitutes holiness and what the Bible means about homosexuality.

The long slow march towards institutional death began, oddly enough, not with a priest, bishop or presiding bishop, but a single homosexual layman by the name of Dr. Louie Crew. He would later change his name to Dr. Louie Crew (Clay) after marrying his partner Ernest Clay. He is now Louie Clay.

Crew founded an organization he called *Integrity* and sent out a newsletter in October 1974, to a few select Episcopalians, postmarked from Fort Valley, the county seat of Peach County, Georgia. The newsletter was called *Integrity: Homosexual Episcopal Forum* and was circulated solely by Crew, then a young homosexual just beginning his career as an English professor.

Almost immediately, Crew received two calls from interested persons; coincidentally, they were both from Chicago although they were strangers to each other, one a priest and the other a lay person. With Crew's encouragement from afar, those two and other homosexuals from Chicago organized the first chapter of *Integrity* during a meeting in December 1974. The following summer, the first national gathering convened in Chicago.

Crew's salary as a young English professor at a small state college was minimal, but he had the benefit of paid airfare to attend seminars and conferences. He would pocket the airfare and travel to the conferences by Greyhound, stopping frequently along the way to network with bishops and others. The road toward full inclusion included bumpy bus rides.

By the 1976 General Convention in Minneapolis, Integrity had spread across the country with chapters in many cities; representatives of Integrity had been well received by official church spokesmen; and church leaders were accommodating to Integrity during the convention. In addition to the momentous revisions to the canons to allow women's ordination to the priesthood, the 1976 General Convention also acted favorably on homosexual measures, including a resolution stating: *that homosexual persons are children of God who have a full and equal claim with all other persons upon the love, acceptance, and pastoral concern and care of the Church.*

A "full and equal claim" is pretty heady stuff, but following the ordination of lesbian Ellen Marie Barrett in January 1977, the pendulum had begun to swing. Big time. Crew called the 1979 General Convention, "the height of homophobia."

No distinction was ever made about *being* a homosexual and *practicing* homosexual behavior. The assumption was that to be a homosexual was in fact to live it out regardless of what Scripture taught. Crew made no effort to hide his homosexual relationship with Clay or engage with Scripture. His efforts were solely to change the Church's direction and thinking with words like "inclusion" and "diversity". Scripture would be relegated to the dust heap of history and he had the full support of his bishop, John Shelby Spong, the bishop of Newark who was on his own journey out of the historic orthodox faith. Satan had gained a foothold and his footprint would in time spread like a cancer throughout the Episcopal Church.

What was once sexual perversion was slowly being legitimized as a lifestyle acceptable to the Church and presumably to God.

In the 1970s as an emerging leader, Crew, now pondered how to institutionalize these social changes within the religious communities that began with the Stonewall Riots. Under the banner of "Integrity" Crew became the leader organizing a cadre of homosexual activists that would in time turn the Episcopal Church upside down.

Crew knew it would be uphill battle especially as he had been raised an evangelical in the Southern Baptist Convention and he would later become a Baptist minister.

But his sexual proclivities won out. He now states that, "All institutional language is a 'put-off' from the spiritual journey." This is deeply ironic in that he would later join the Episcopal Church which is full of "institutional language."

Crew left his life as a Baptist minister behind and became an agnostic but would later join The Episcopal Church. At the same time Crew says he struggled to deal with his sexual feelings and decided to affirm his homosexuality by coming out. Crew described this as a "personal and intimate" spiritual experience. He states, "Coming out to yourself is the most important. You don't treat yourself as a mechanism."

Scripture was firmly on the backburner of his mind as he thrust forward his homosexuality to a world, he believed, was ready to receive it. His timing was close to perfect. The culture was slowly moving his way and he quickly jumped onto the bandwagon dragging the Episcopal Church along with him.

This interpretation of Scripture was and is a gross departure from both his Baptist upbringing and from scripture itself. Nowhere does Scripture teach that "coming out" is to be "born again"; that is a gross misrepresentation and exegesis of a text that evangelists like Billy Graham pleaded with sinners to turn from, embrace purity of life and trust God for their salvation. Crew turned biblical sexuality on its head, following his own "devices and desires" justifying it all in the name of his new-fangled doctrine of inclusion.

Crew got his sexual foot in the episcopal door in 1974 when he and his partner, Ernest Clay, moved to San Francisco and found a sympathetic hearing at Grace Cathedral offices where Bishop James Pike, the Episcopal Church's first serious heretical bishop presided in the mid-1960s.

Crew called it right, his experience there confirmed that the Episcopal Church would be a welcoming home for homosexual persons.

In 1974, Crew began his grass-roots group *Integrity* that continues to this day working for the full inclusion of lesbian, homosexual, bisexual and transgender people in the Episcopal Church. The Church had gone from thoroughly heterosexual to pansexual in one generation. It was a feat that present day cultural Marxists could only stand back and admire.

In December of 1974, the first *Integrity* group met in the apartment of a Chicago priest. Crew writes, "A joke popular in the Episcopal Church at that time asked: 'How many straight priests in the diocese of Chicago does it take to put in a light bulb? Answer: Both of them.'"(2)

Crew and Integrity set about knocking on doors, writing letters, and making their presence known as "lesbigay."(3) He writes of their growing numbers. From 1976-1984, Integrity had about 1,200 members. In 1995, the number had grown to 2,500 members. Today *Integrity* is organized through over 60 chapters across the nation. Integrity's chapters are groups of 10 or more members in an area or diocese who gather monthly or quarterly to promote welcome and inclusion in their areas.

Crew acknowledges that the open political structure of the Episcopal Church allowed his organization to participate and lobby successfully for the inclusion of homosexuals. He writes, "Many of the same persons who shaped the Constitution of the United States shaped the Constitution of the Episcopal Church."(5)

Crew's successful strategizing eventually helped lead to the 2003 consecration of the homosexual bishop, Gene Robinson, a man who would cause the Episcopal Church to split leading to the formation of the Anglican Church in North America.

Few bishops challenged his sexual perversion. Crew's charm, academic qualifications and push, push, push paid off. Most bishops had been poorly theologically educated in liberal Episcopal seminaries where Scripture and Biblical interpretation was never high in the curricula. They were susceptible to Crew's charm, and plea for inclusion quickly struck a sympathetic chord with them. They were easy targets for Crew and Integrity. Priests who were trained in liberal theological seminaries were an even easier target. Inclusion and diversity easily won out with them.

His political maneuvering and machinations paid off. Crew himself admitted; "One of the reasons lesbians and homosexuals have succeeded in the Episcopal Church is that we spend time learning how it operates, and then we teach one another."(5)

The name of the game was political; Scripture, history, and tradition had been dispensed with. Little or no thought was given about how all this would impact the broader Anglican Communion. Pansexual narcissism had engulfed the Episcopal Church. There would be no going back.

Integrity now claimed a highly respected place in the Episcopal Church. Crew writes; "Integrity began to wield real influence at the 1988 General Convention. Friends and foes alike credited us as having the best network at the convention." (6)

It was the triumph of politics over faith and the doctrine of the church and the teaching of Scripture.

Crew and other like-minded thinkers now planned on how they would modify Episcopal tradition in order that homosexuals would be included at every level in the church. Crew's new mantra was, "We have not been living in sin. The Church has."

Truth had now been turned completely on its head. There would be little talk of Scripture's prohibition against sodomy or sexual sin of any kind. The shiv was in.

Crew exercised leadership in defining justice for homosexuals (or to use his terminology lesbigay,) as a civil rights struggle. When asked about this, Crew responded, "Of course it is a civil rights issue." It was no longer a Biblical issue or Scripture's authority to determine truth.

Not everyone agreed with him. Crew points to his active foes saying that the "Radical Right has mounted a regressive reaction." It was "regressive" only because Crew had labeled those opposing him for lacking inclusion, not because they opposed his behavior on biblical grounds.

At the time of the interview, Louie said that he and his husband plan to have a legal civil ceremony within a few years. He describes marriage as "a commitment forever. Marriage is a wonderful institution if you see it as a living and organic thing."

Crew had abandoned the sacred understanding of marriage between a man and a woman and redefined it to suit his own sexual proclivities, attempting to overturn 2,000 years of Church teaching. It was no small undertaking, but Crew and his *Integrity* gang were determined to do it.

Others in political life also saw the need for changing the position of homosexual people in the Episcopal Church and quietly began their own odyssey as they sought acceptance for other emerging sexualities like bi-sexuality and transgenderism.

The murder of a homosexual California politician was a turning point and galvanized many, including some Episcopalians, to seek civil rights for homosexuals. Many felt stung into awareness that they too needed to publicly acknowledge their homosexuality and demand that society accept them.

As the *Integrity* organization grew, Crew organized the first *Integrity* group in Chicago and from there the burgeoning movement multiplied quickly. His goal was to bring homosexuality out of the closet in the Episcopal Church through groups planted all over the country.

Crew points out that some bishops who supported *Integrity* were elected Presiding Bishop, including the Rt. Rev. Edmond Browning in 1985. In 1992 Browning delivered the main address at the *Integrity* National Convention. Crew got full support for his homosexuality from Presiding Bishops Frank Griswold, later Katharine Jefferts Schori, and more recently Michael Curry, the Episcopal Church's first Black Presiding Bishop.

According to Crew, *Integrity* supported the election of the first female bishop in the Episcopal Church in 1989, the Rt. Rev. Barbara Harris.

He states that an umbrella group of organizations, including *Integrity*, supported Harris.

To Crew's mind, the elevation of women to the episcopacy and the liberation of homosexuals went in tandem. Keeping women from the highest ranks of the church was considered repressive; keeping homosexuals from all orders of ministry in the Church was oppressive and homophobic. Crew had the perfect segue to push the Church along a revisionist pathway into what he hoped would be a church liberated from what he considered its racist, sexist, repressive past and into a future of unbridled joy and hope.

That proved not to be the case. His actions proved divisive and ultimately destructive. His twin mantras "joy everybody" and "God loves absolutely everybody" sounded good, but inside the velvet glove lay the iron fist of full inclusion and he would stop at nothing to achieve his goal.

Crew correctly identified an important issue in this controversy. Many disagree about what constitutes holiness and what the Bible means about homosexuality.

As Crew's power within the Church grew, his hatred towards any opposition also grew. One such group was the American Anglican Council, led at the time by the Rev. Canon David Anderson, a group that became the loyal opposition to The Episcopal Church. Crew hated them. At one point he blasted the AAC and said this:

"The dirty tricks at Watergate did not bring Richard Nixon down. He did that himself by denying his association with the plot once The Washington Post brought it to light. Any leader of AAC who wants to survive in a position of vital influence in TEC should leave the AAC and apologize for the harm the dirty tricks have done to all, not just to TEC and the communion, but to faithful people with genuine dissent."

Crew became so powerful that by 2006, it was he and he alone who was given the privilege of interviewing nominees to be the next Presiding Bishop.

The list of candidates had to answer two questions: if a homosexual or lesbian person is elected on your watch, would you consent to the election? If a homosexual or lesbian person is elected on your watch, would you be willing to serve as key consecrator?

Of the seven candidates just one was a woman, Katharine Jefferts Schori, Bishop of Nevada. She was overwhelmingly elected the 26th Presiding Bishop of the Episcopal Church. Outgoing Presiding Frank Griswold, said at the time, "The decision today is the fruit of the witness and ministry of women bishops, priests, and deacons in the life of our church." It was also the fruit of years of hard labor put in by one layman – Dr. Louie Crew. Secure in his knowledge that he was more powerful than almost any bishop, Crew turned his attention to the Marriage Canons of the Church which he sought to change. He was again successful.

In 1973 the ECUSA changed its doctrine of marriage by changing its canon law and then set forth this new understanding of matrimony in its marriage service within its official Prayer Book of 1979.

The purpose of marriage, officially understood, was said to be in the mutual relation of the man and woman and the procreation of children. This would now be presented as optional and not a requirement of the Lord. In other words, the received teaching of the Church of man and woman united as one flesh for procreation and nurturing a family was made optional, as was the understanding that marriage is for life, "until death do us part."

This novel situation was taken for granted in the ECUSA where whether one was divorced and remarried was not a question in standing for church office or seeking ordination.

In one stroke in 2006 both the agenda of the homosexual groups and the erroneous doctrine of the 1973 Canon and the 1979 marriage service came together in a resolution from the diocese of Newark, Crew's diocese. The resolution requested that the marriage service of the 1979 book be used for same sex couples (where civil law permits) and that within it, man/woman or husband/wife be simply changed to two persons.

The resolution read:

> Resolved, the House of _______ concurring, That this 75th General Convention authorizes use of the rites for Celebration and Blessing of a Marriage and The Blessing of a Civil Marriage in "the Book of Common Prayer (1979)" for same-sex couples in those civil jurisdictions that permit same-sex marriage, and further authorizes modification of gender references in the rites to accommodate such marriages.

For Crew this was yet another victorious milestone along the pathway to full acceptance of homosexuality. He wrote:

> This does not constitute a revision of the Prayer Book but would instead be simply an adaptation. It would be similar to the allowance of the use of feminine terms in the rite for the Ordering of Deacons in the 1928 Book of Common Prayer. Women were ordained to the diaconate beginning in 1968 despite the language of the 1928 text which was exclusively male (both in the rite itself and in the rubrics and preface), which language was not modified until the authorization of the current Book of Common Prayer in 1979.

One commentator noted that Crew and his small but committed group of homosexuals and lesbians set as a goal the transformation of the Episcopal Church into an institution which would be a safe haven for uninhibited homosexuals to pursue their proclivities without being subject to judgement, criticism or moral constraint. Their strategy was simple:

1. First and foremost terrorize the traditionalists by labeling them bigots and homophobes. Central in this was the duty to wail unceasingly "homophobia" at anyone who even remotely questioned their goals.

2. Pretend that their real goal was to create a "kinder, gentler and inclusive" church, which would be tolerant of homosexuals and lesbians, when in fact their goal was to take over the Episcopal power structure in order to protect their interests. "Kinder, gentler and inclusive" was guaranteed to produce a generally positive response from most

traditionalists and crack the door open to achieving their more radical aims.

3. Infiltrate the seminaries over an extended period with steadily increasing numbers of homosexuals and lesbians, until a tipping point was achieved when those in favor of their agenda overbalanced those opposed to it and moved out into the wider clergy environment in their respective dioceses. Again, cries of "homophobia" against their opponents were the order of the day. (The term "Gay Mafia" was to become increasingly common in the seminaries).

4. Downplay the importance of family creation and support, and the nurturing of children, and make same-sex unions and homosexual marriage the top priority, while insisting that all children be made aware of the homosexual lifestyle, and wherever possible be encouraged to choose it.

5. Ridicule and slander any group which ministers to unhappy or suicidal homosexuals by using the premise that through the grace of Jesus Christ they could change.

6. Restructure the theology of the church to a format that could be happily accepted by homosexuals and lesbians, by revising, censoring, parsing and ridiculing the Holy Scriptures' references to homosexuality wherever and whenever possible. Make sure that this approach is used in the seminaries.

7. Take over the National Executive Council, and if possible, the office of the Presiding Bishop.

On all these issues Louie Crew was successful using both charm and aggressive tactics by his multi-person Integrity lobbying team before important votes at General Conventions, tipping the scales in the House of Bishops, and House of Deputies to the point where they would approve an active homosexual bishop, and hopefully elect a Presiding Bishop completely favorable to the Lesbigay agenda.

Over time, as he aged, Crew withdrew from the lobbying and political structures of the Episcopal Church confident in the knowledge that he had won the day. He had achieved all his goals and therefore it was no longer important to his cause to update his blog through the 2006 Convention.

He had forced the traditionalist and orthodox elements in the church to either capitulate, conform, or abandon the Episcopal Church. Many would leave for more Biblical pastures, believing that any sexual act outside of marriage between a man and a woman was sexual sin. Now also came the firing of priests, suing them using church funds, properties being taken over, and ultimately the withdrawal of whole dioceses from the Episcopal Church. It was an inglorious victory for one man.

Years later Crew would admit that the Bible was not sympathetic to homosexuality. It never changed his outlook or mind.

With Crew, the seduction of the Episcopal Church had begun in earnest and he would be forever recognized, perhaps even canonized as its foremost cheerleader. Bishops and presiding bishops would fall all over themselves to embrace his worldview, aided and abetted by an increasingly sympathetic secular culture.

Dr. Louie Crew had defined and changed the Episcopal Church forever, there would be no going back. Only the judgement of God now remained.

PRESIDING BISHOP EDMOND LEE BROWNING

An Angry Leader for an Angry Time

Be angry and sin not. Eph. 4: 26

In 1985, Bishop Edmond Lee Browning seized the reins of power as Presiding Bishop. He was the first of a new wave of post-modern bishops to take the helm of the Episcopal Church.

Browning set to work re-structuring the Episcopal Church to allow the ordination of homosexuals and lesbians. He thought of his work as having "no outcasts", but it soon became apparent that Browning himself created a whole class of outcasts within the Episcopal Church. Browning's outcasts were those who wished to stay true to the Bible and to Biblical authority on faith and morals.

Browning committed himself entirely to his "new" agenda - the ordination of homosexuals and lesbians into the Episcopal Church, thus ending 2,000 years of church history, tradition and faith, bringing on a crisis from which the Church has never recovered.

In 1992, Browning delivered the main address at the *Integrity National Convention* in Houston, Texas, embracing homosexuality. From that time forward he fought continually for the ordination of homosexuals.

It was a dramatic pastoral visit. Browning issued a strong clarion call to lesbian and homosexual Episcopalians to "keep the faith" and to continue to "tell their stories" in a church, he said, that sometimes does not want to listen.

"You've got to know how important it is for you to hang in," Browning told some 200 members of *Integrity*.

Browning's presence at the *Integrity* convention was the first by a presiding bishop of the Episcopal Church. The visit took place almost exactly a year after a highly contentious General Convention in Phoenix recognized the ambiguity Episcopalians had in addressing the issue of homosexuality.

The new catchword would be "dialogue".

In 1994, Browning approved of Bishop John Spong's *Koinonia Statement* fully supporting the ordination of homosexuals. Nearly one hundred bishops signed the statement, including Browning and the future Presiding Bishop Frank Tracy Griswold.

Clearly these two bishops, Browning and Spong, had decided this was a fight they would and could win and they went full speed ahead. The faster they went, the larger the group of outcasts became. Browning's initial goal became a pointless slogan with new divisions and broken relationships springing up everywhere.

The then Archbishop of Canterbury, George Carey, called this statement a "bombshell." Browning and Spong had bombed the Biblical standards and the Christian tradition. And although many still revered the Archbishop of Canterbury as a spiritual guide, Browning led the Episcopal Church into full rebellion against Carey. When Carey visited the US, he was met at every turn with people coached into telling Carey to accept homosexual ordination and to listen to the stories of activist homosexuals and lesbians. Carey understood this was the conditioning that Browning put into place.

Carey wrote poignantly that he could not bless that which God would not bless.

The conflicts within the House of Bishops boiled over and Spong began yelling "Homophobe!" at Bishop John MacNaughton from the Diocese of West Texas. Browning supported Spong even after this public abuse and the ordinations that Browning and Spong wanted began happening.

The first ordination of a noncelibate homosexual went unbelievably badly. Spong ordained Robert Williams in 1989, an openly homosexual man with AIDS, living with a male partner. The narrative did not go as planned, with Williams announcing that neither celibacy nor monogamy were natural to human beings. Spong pretended great shock at this statement. Spong put pressure on Williams, who finally resigned his ordination. Williams later died of AIDS.

Browning, it was soon to be revealed, was the child of an alcoholic father.

Through this mutual knowledge, the two bishops Browning and Spong bonded with one another to change, challenge and chastise the Episcopal Church and Anglican Communion. They saw each other's problems and decided that structural change in the Episcopal Church was what was needed.

In doing so, they abandoned the authority of Scripture and with it the fear of the Lord, the hope of heaven and left the dread of hell far behind. They detached the creation accounts and ontology of sexuality, and in time, the salvation Christ offered.

As a further sign and symbol of Browning's ineptness, in early 1994, Browning asked The Bishop of the Diocese of Northwestern Pennsylvania, Donald Davis, to step down following allegations that the late bishop sexually abused four girls in the 1970s and 1980s.

Bishop Davis was forced to resign from the House of Bishops (in which bishops still retain their membership even if retired), to refrain from any priestly or episcopal duties; to undergo pastoral counseling; and to see a psychiatrist. Davis was removed as a bishop of the church. However, Browning did not make his abuse public; that silence would later come back to bite him.

The sordid mess erupted fully in 2010 when the Rt. Rev. Sean Rowe learned of the abuse and offered an abject apology to Bishop Davis' victims, their families and everyone whose trust in the church had been violated. He asked for their forgiveness.

Years later, when Charles E. Bennison, Bishop of Pennsylvania faced trial for fraud and failure to report his brother's sexual abuse of a minor. Bennison pleaded he should be reinstated because former Presiding Bishop Edmond Browning wasn't removed [from office] for keeping silent about Bishop Davis. Sin has a nasty way of catching up with one.

In September 2009, some 263 Episcopal clergy including 20 Episcopal bishops, signed a declaration on sexual morality, justice and healing. The signers, including Browning, argued that sexuality is God's life-giving and life-fulfilling gift. "We come from diverse religious communities to recognize sexuality as central to our humanity and as integral to our spirituality. We are speaking out against the pain, brokenness, oppression, and loss of meaning that many experience about their sexuality." The declaration was a puff piece for the full acceptance of pansexuality.

"Our culture needs a sexual ethic focused on personal relationships and social justice rather than particular sexual acts. All persons have the right and responsibility to lead sexual lives that express love, justice, mutuality, commitment, consent, and pleasure. Grounded in respect for the body and for the vulnerability that intimacy brings, this ethic fosters physical, emotional, and spiritual health. It accepts no double standards and applies to all persons, without regard to sex, gender, color, age, bodily condition, marital status, or sexual orientation."

Browning was not above mocking even his own tradition. In North Carolina on the occasion of the consecration of the Rev James Gary Gloster as suffragan bishop in the Episcopal Diocese of North Carolina in Duke University's chapel, nine splendidly vested bishops took part, including Episcopal Presiding Bishop Edmond Browning, and then proceeded to stick big red noses on themselves.

Following the presentation of traditional elements of a bishop's garb - pectoral cross, crozier, miter - a group of clowns and children, 'symbolizing the importance of laughter and play and faith,' came forward to present their gifts. At this point, reported *The (Durham) Herald-Sun*, a clown put a red nose on the new suffragan, and Gloster, 'who enjoys humor and clowning...turned to the bishops standing behind him and stuck big red noses on many of them, including Browning, who smiled broadly through the unexpected turn of events.

Browning also had taken part in at least one other bit of intra-ritual 'comic relief.' A college graduate who attended an Episcopal Youth Event in Missoula, Montana, several years ago told The *Christian Challenge* magazine editor Auburn Traycik that after Browning appeared in full episcopal regalia to celebrate Holy Communion for the gathering, he pulled a 'super-soaker' out from under his cope and squirted the now excited congregation of young people, later reassuring them that they had been 'blessed': reportedly, the super-soaker contained holy water.

Browning was also not above passing over the sins of a bishop when it suited him. The late Bishop of Navajoland, Steven T. Plummer, a married man, was reported in 1993 to have admitted to sexual activity with his nephew, a male minor over a period of some two years, ending around 1989.

When Browning heard about it, he sent Plummer away for a year of therapy, and then returned him to service as bishop, based on his counselors' opinions that he was unlikely to repeat his former behavior. The victim in the case was no longer a minor and "unwilling to pursue this any further," Browning said in 1993.

At the time in 1994 Plummer was reinstated, reports emerged that Native American members and the Council of Navajoland were divided on the bishop's return. Still, Plummer gained the support of Browning and the Episcopal House of Bishops to continue leading the Mission. Plummer died of cancer in 2005 at the age of 60.

Money Crisis

Browning gave tremendous power to a woman, Ellen F. Cooke, 52, who cared for the finances of the denomination. A college dropout from Virginia, she rose to become the powerful treasurer of the national Episcopal Church. During her tenure, she embezzled $1.5 million from the church and evaded $300,000 in income taxes. Cooke took the Episcopal Church to the cleaners under Browning's watch. Laurie Goodstein of the *Washington Post* described it as the largest embezzlement in mainline church history.

For eight years, Cooke was the most influential female lay official at Episcopal Church headquarters in Manhattan, responsible for handling millions in church investments and trusts, and administering the church's operating budget. Her steady embezzlement went unnoticed until Cooke moved from Montclair, N.J., to McLean, Va., with her husband, Nicholas T. Cooke, when he was made rector of the prominent St. John's Episcopal Church there.

Ellen Cooke's theft, believed to be the largest ever from a mainline Protestant church, cracked open fault lines in a 2.5 million-member denomination riven by theological disputes over the ordination of women and homosexuals. Many conservatives used the financial scandal as another reason to call for the ouster of the liberal-leaning Browning, who had hired Cooke and shielded her from early criticism. Cooke's stealing from Browning's own discretionary fund made him directly and personally responsible, unlike the other sources of her thievery.

In 1996, Cooke was sentenced to five years in prison despite her claim that a psychiatric disorder caused her to embezzle. U.S. District Judge Maryanne Trump Barry, her voice edged with outrage, rejected Cooke's claim of having no memory of diverting funds over a period of five years because of mental illness. She also stated that Browning had defended Cooke from early criticism. Some called for Browning's removal as Presiding Bishop.

Browning seemed not to have paid attention to rules of any kind, whether they came from the Bible about how we should live or from accepted accounting practices and manuals or even from church canons. Whenever Browning was in the house, rules took wings and flew out the window.

Ellen Cooke was no petty thief. She had large designs. She embezzled over $2 million dollars, including hundreds of thousands from the Presiding Bishop's own discretionary fund over a number of years. There were no checks and balances.

Nothing ever seemed to work out for Browning, with Spong's debacle becoming Browning's debacle and Cooke's debacle becoming Browning's debacle.

Browning's accomplishments included the following:

- An extraordinarily angry first ordination of an active homosexual clergyman in the person of Robert Williams.
- A scene where Browning's friend Spong abused another bishop.
- Open disregard for Archbishop of Canterbury George Carey, a truly caring man who was popular in this country until Browning attempted to turn him.
- The largest embezzlement in church history.
- A steadily growing group of outcasts that finally ended up protesting Browning's leadership.

This is not a list of accomplishments that anyone would want to have or see on a resumé.

The question became where did Browning come from and how did he rise to this position with what appeared to be an obvious lack of gifts and standards. Some of the answers to this question comes from his devotional manual.

True to form, Browning dismissed the accepted route of a memoir and included his history in a spiritual document he called a devotional.

Browning's devotional book, *A Year of Days with the Book of Common Prayer,* reads like a minefield of personal anger and disappointments. Browning mixes together in chaotic fashion his fragmented history, numerous angry comments opposing the Religious Right and his odd theological leanings.

His "memoir" for his faithful followers yielded only three messages.

He didn't believe in a personal relationship with Jesus Christ.

He also no longer believed in the authority of the Bible.

His childhood was very sad and he will tell you what happened if you keep reading his book. He was aware that his life had destroyed a lot of the Christian faith.

On the second "message" he had this to say which explains his inexplicable behavior. "My father was an alcoholic. I cannot recall a time when he was not afflicted. . . His addiction would reduce him to staying alone in his room for days at a time. The sorrow of this resided permanently in our house."

Browning describes himself as a boy watching his drunken and mute father stagger to the bathroom. Browning never felt healed from this situation. He revealed that therapists said he must be angry. At no time was he invited to forgive his father. On reading his "memoir", one can feel his anger and rage.

Browning came up with the odd notion that the anger that went deep within him became God's healing power within. However, such anger never became a healing force. He ignored the biblical warning found in James 1: 20 which said, "Human anger does not produce the righteousness that God desires."

Browning did not see it that way.

"People...in the world of therapy have often told me that I must be angry about my early life with my dad. . . There is absolutely no doubt that my father's enslavement to alcohol affected everyone in my family very powerfully. . . "

He goes on to say that it didn't feel like anger, but the healing touch of God. He never therefore entirely admits the anger and never testifies to a healing from his anger, yet he says that he thinks that the anger became the healing touch of God.

This detachment from reality would continue throughout his ministry. Browning clearly never knew healing. He talks about addiction to anger and how a "well-placed zinger" is both exciting and feels good and "better than the painful, halting process of dialogue could ever feel. A direct hit. A bull's-eye. A victory over the enemy."

Browning's ministry was tainted, filled with anger and self-righteous indignation, with the result that he loved attacking his enemies.

Browning also said that he loved victims, but this seemed to reflect the victimization he felt in his own home situation.

It was natural then for him to take up the cause of homosexual ordinations, seeing such persons as victims in need of protection from allegedly heterosexual homophobes and haters. Browning was angry at what had happened to him, angry at traditional American life, angry at the way things were done. Just angry.

And that's not a good place to be in for ministry.

The truth began to emerge; his anger and unresolved issues made him an unstable leader. He attacked the historic Christian faith and began its vast deconstruction. Browning's legacy is his open deconstruction of the Episcopal Church, the first presiding bishop to do so.

C. S. Lewis said self-pity can lead to the lust for revenge. Browning, full of anger at his father, tore down the Bible with its history of patriarchy, which meant for him the stories about Old Testament leaders, prophets and patriarchs…stories about the fathers of Israel and the prophets they hearkened to and often disobeyed.

Big problems were soon spotted in his *Devotional!*

Browning writes; "Sunday at eleven o'clock is the most segregated hour in the American week." Browning did not say this, Martin Luther King Jr. did. There was no attribution. Scholars get fired for that kind of thing, but Browning was no scholar. Even though he deconstructed the Christian faith out of his own felt pain, he felt no qualms claiming King's quote without sourcing it.

King preached this at the Washington National Cathedral on March 31, 1968, and on April 4, 1968, he was assassinated. Browning leaves the quote hanging as if he had written it.

Browning just keeps on ticking without turning back to see if ethical standards are being applied anywhere. He never mentions that this is not his quote.

In his book, Browning regularly throws stones at what he calls the Religious Right. Browning ridiculed a church in Southern Maryland in the Diocese of Washington. Browning's outcasts are innumerable.

Many wondered about his lack of compassion. What happened to compassion when it came to the Religious Right? There was none.

Where did it go?

Did Browning's compassion dry up like a raisin in the sun when he thought about Southern Maryland and the Religious Right? Or all of the Anglican Communion he was trying to push around by his blind antics?

The Theology of Presiding Bishop Browning

What was the basic image that Browning proposed for the Christian faith?

Browning writes that we are NOT for any reason to interpret the Hebrew Scriptures as a forerunner or foretaste of Christ.

"I imagine you feel the same reluctance I do to force Christian concepts back onto the Hebrew Scriptures." He called this, "Robbing the Jewish people of their integrity by projecting its explicit expectation backward upon their sacred texts."

Of course, if we stop using the Hebrew Scriptures, we stop reading the New Testament because the writers of the New Testament used the Hebrew Scriptures repeatedly so they could understand this wonderful and joyful mystery of the Incarnation.

That seemed to be Browning's entire plan. We are no longer to read about God the Father and God the Son anymore. Instead, he adopted Spong's vague idea that some mystic consciousness might exist and because of this, we should entirely repudiate the Hebrew Scriptures.

No more Old Testament for Browning. No more Jewish law. No more prophecies. Instead, the Episcopal Church would focus on social conditioning and engineering, concentrating on supporting an endless array of social issues, because for Browning, the historic Christian faith was no more. His understanding of the resurrection, for example, became "a permanent puzzle."

Browning's life seemed like a permanent puzzle with the resurrection no longer relevant, its place of power and hope and rejoicing shattered and gone.

Browning does show a method, however. He writes; "The fastest way to destroy a people is to destroy its memory. That has been understood by despots and dictators throughout the history of humankind, and so the eradication of memories has always been an enterprise of tyrants: stamp out the indigenous language, stamp out the indigenous names, educate the children in the traditions of the conqueror and not in their own traditions, and resistance to our rule will die out in one generation."

Browning knew this and admits it.

Browning destroyed the Bible as the Church's source of authority and threw the Old Testament out the window. He wrote, "Stamp out the Bible and the Christian faith disappears before our eyes." He threw orthodox Christianity under the bus.

Browning was not ignorant of the impact of his attempting to destroy the Christian memory of the Hebrew Scriptures. He knew that this would destroy people's confidence in Scripture…and he did it in one generation. One is forced to ask, was this his plan all along?

Browning's sad legacy included supporting Bishop Spong in the ordination of an activist homosexual to the priesthood, HE stopped using the Hebrew Scriptures to explain the identity of Jesus Christ in the name of protecting the integrity of the Jewish people. He presided over the largest church embezzlement of all time by his treasurer, Browning denounced the idea of a personal relationship with Jesus Christ, echoes of which we would later hear repeated from another presiding bishop - Katharine Jefferts Schori.

The Episcopal Church would now begin its sad, pathetic disappearing act under a man with unresolved anger issues.

Browning seemed to understand that he worked for the agenda of others and was not motivated by his own faith or lack of it. His dry *Devotional Manual* reads like a confessional. Browning writes, "Suppose we get caught up in an agenda that we truly believe to be the will of God for us and then later find out we made a mistake? Or suppose we never find that out, and we go to our graves mistaken, on the wrong track?"

The 24th Presiding Bishop and Primate of the Episcopal Church, Edmond Lee Browning, died on July 11, 2016, with the Church's agenda firmly in place having taken over his ministry and ultimately destroying it.

Browning tore out whole chunks of gospel truth and left others to pick up the pieces.

C. S. Lewis warned in his book *The Abolition of Man*, that when the Way disappears, humanity itself will be abolished.

The slow abolition of the Episcopal Church had begun. Under Frank Griswold, the pace would now quicken and the deconstruction continue. The church had been seduced one more time by a man singularly unfit to run a major denomination.

PRESIDING BISHOP FRANK TRACY GRISWOLD

Frank Tracy Griswold was born in Bryn Mawr, Pennsylvania on Philadelphia's Blue Blood Main Line. He was educated at St Paul's School in Concord, New Hampshire, and earned a Bachelor of Arts (B.A.) in English literature from Harvard College. He attended the General Theological Seminary where he earned another Bachelor of Arts degree in theology (subsequently converted to Master of Arts) at Oriel College, Oxford University.

He was ordained a priest in 1963 and then served at three parishes in Pennsylvania until his nomination as Bishop of Chicago, a position he held from 1987 until he became the Presiding Bishop in 1998.

He was a member of the Standing Committee for the 1998 Lambeth Conference which produced Resolution 1:10, the litmus test for sexuality in the Anglican Communion that Griswold deplored. As time revealed, his tenure was the most disastrous and fateful of all the Presiding Bishops.

Griswold's tenure as Presiding Bishop of the Episcopal Church was marked by a history of broken promises, bad theology, the push for full homosexual acceptance, Eastern mysticism and a rapidly declining Church.

When Griswold ascended the throne to become the 25th Presiding Bishop of the Episcopal Church in July, 1997, in Philadelphia, following much hot politicking, he promised to unite church members and usher in a new age of tolerance, offering enlightened progressive views that would carry the church into the new millennium.

He told the story about how God had spoken to him in Italy as he visited the significant sites of the life and witness of Francis of Assisi. He said that God told him to "Rebuild His Church."

He went on to say that he wanted to be a reconciler between conservatives and liberals and pledged to be "a presiding bishop who belongs to all."

Most felt that Virginia Bishop, Peter James Lee, was destined to be the next Presiding Bishop. At the last minute, Lee unexpectedly pulled out of the election. Rumors ran rampant about Lee's withdrawal, revolving around his own sexual preferences, which called into question his potential leadership. Following Lee's withdrawal, Bishop Frank Griswold of the Diocese of Chicago won the election.

Griswold seemed like a panacea needed at a crucial time following Browning's nonstop anger. It was generally known that priests were glad to see the back of Griswold in Chicago, and his elevation to Presiding Bishop brought sighs of relief in the Midwest windy city.

At the time of his consecration, Katie Sherrod, a liberal woman activist from the Diocese of Ft. Worth and vice president of the Episcopal Women's Caucus, said, "I think he will continue the philosophy that there are no outcasts in this church." She called him someone capable of providing the "kind of balance that is sorely needed in the church."

However, Bishop John W. Howe of the Diocese of Central Florida, said at the time, Griswold has "as his first order of business reaching out to those on the other side of the great divide. If he does not do that, it is hard to see how these two constituencies will continue under one roof."

In his sermon at his installation, Griswold called on Episcopalians to be better listeners, to treat each other with respect, and to have a "compassionate heart ... capable of rebuilding the church in the service of the Gospel for the sake of the world."

At his first press conference, Griswold said that "the ministry of the presiding bishop is to stand at the center." When asked whether he would offer some hope to conservatives who feel marginalized, he said, "I hope I am orthodox in my theology. All of us have truth to tell." He said that "the church is destined always to contain diametrically opposing views" and part of his task is to "help the different voices hear one another" through continuing conversation. "I see myself as an Anglican with the breadth to live with ambiguity and contradicting perspectives and stay grounded."

"Discovering truth and catholicity is what I commit myself to as presiding bishop," he said. Pointing out that conversation and conversion have the same root, meaning to turn or be turned, he added, "We are designed to discover truth together through conversation."

"Conversion is a sacred enterprise in which I am turned around, I am changed by making room for, by considering, by being hospitable toward the opinions, the word, the lived and incarnate truth of another." Griswold said later in a sermon at the closing Eucharist, "Left to our own devices, we are critical, fearful and protective of our own take on truth." Through Jesus Christ and the Holy Spirit, he said, we can "welcome the paradox, complexity, ambiguity and outright contradiction, which is where real life is lived and the grace and peace of God are truly to be found."

In his first major statement, he said that, broadly speaking, the Episcopal Church is in conflict with Scripture. "The only way to justify it is to say, well, Jesus talks about the Spirit guiding the church and guiding believers and bringing to their awareness things they cannot deal with yet. So, one would have to say that the mind of Christ operative in the church over time . . . has led the church to, in effect, contradict the words of the Gospels," he told the *Philadelphia Inquirer.*

It was a statement that would come back to haunt him over the years, yet this statement accurately reflected Griswold's own conflicted theology. He correctly perceived a huge divide between the scriptural witness to the gospel message and what he believed to be the mind of Christ. Griswold decided that the mind of Christ was a conglomeration of worldly culture, social confusion, and Islamic beliefs couched in mystical language, though this was, in fact, the mind of a declining western culture. Griswold's corrupt theological confusion grew, reaching its apogee in the formal consecration of V. Gene Robinson, the openly homoerotic, non-celibate Bishop of New Hampshire. It was, for Griswold, the triumph of pluriformity. It also signaled the beginning of the end of The Episcopal Church, the final 100-yard dash in pursuit of 40 years of pansexual acceptance.

Years later in an interview, he admitted that the complexity of leadership drove him to a deeper place of prayer. "I realized that I didn't have, from my own imagination and skillsets, the competency to oversee the complexity of a diocese or a national church institution."

Griswold's Rhetoric

Griswold spoke great rhetoric. He spoke in beautiful terms of Episcopalians having 'Christ consciousness' and going beyond good and evil and right and wrong, glossed with international perspectives and multidimensional thinking and other high-sounding transcendent phrases. He loved mystical icons and consciousness-raising Islamic poetry and he enjoyed globe-trotting. He hated giving up being Presiding Bishop. He admits he cried the day he had to leave office.

If the goal of language is to actually speak something meaningful, Griswold failed miserably. No one knew exactly what he was saying. The name of the rhetorical device Griswold used is called "The Wall of Text". Nick Milne defines this wall of text, "In which the vacuity of your position is obscured by intense and impenetrable verbiage."

Griswold tossed numerous quotes and buzzwords at the reader, even though they were meaningless, but readers felt uncomfortable for saying so. It was at the 1998 Lambeth Conference when Griswold uttered his now famous line that he believed in "pluriform truths", startling then Archbishop of Canterbury, George Carey, and causing the media to scratch its collective head, pondering what he meant. He threw around the term without ever saying what it or he meant by the words. Griswold's political skills included never letting anyone know much of what he thought.

One goal of this 'Wall of Text' was to build a wall between the Christian faith and the new spirituality Griswold actually endorsed. This wall would be so high that no Episcopalian could look over it and see the former Christian faith. Instead, Griswold put in place floating words and phrases that masked his new Sufi Islamic ideas.

Griswold said that we now lived in a post-Christian age and people would no longer believe in the Christian faith as traditionally understood, so he created his own pseudo-Christian universe of vocabulary, using language that could be interpreted in many ways. It regrettably led to mass confusion. Few Episcopalians asked what the words meant because in doing so they felt stupid, which is precisely what Griswold wanted. It kept him in the driver's seat making the questioner feel small and ignorant.

His message was not remotely the gospel or even Scripture. Though his vocabulary sounded wise, his own ideas deconstructed the gospel, covering up what his actual legacy became.

Frank Griswold set about destroying the Episcopal Church and the Anglican Communion as we know it. In its place, he put a disdain for the Bible and for all Christians who still tried to live by it.

Griswold cried unity even as his actions bespoke disunity. He so angered many of his fellow bishops, orthodox priests and laity, that all the documents, statements and letters combined would fill a sizeable book.

One of the worst examples was the public humiliation he brought on the Episcopal Church in statements he made about the United States and the former President of the United States, George W. Bush, following the tragic events of 9/11.

He blamed America and its foreign policies for the events of 9/11, rather than placing the blame on Islamic fundamentalists and Al Qaeda where they belong. He got then Archbishop Rowan Williams, who happened to be in New York City at the time, to agree with him.

When bombings occurred in London in July 2005, sometimes referred to as 7/7, both Archbishop Williams and Griswold weighed in on the terror attacks. The two world Anglican leaders fell short in declaring the terrorist bombings in London acts of Jihadist Muslim murderers. They quickly endorsed ecumenical relations with Islam and Muslim leaders, with Griswold indulging in a statement of Western self-loathing and guilt.

Archbishop of Canterbury George Carey and Presiding Bishop Griswold

As early as 1994, Griswold was one of 80 bishops who signed a statement arguing that sexual orientation is "morally neutral" and that "faithful, monogamous, committed" homosexual relationships should be accepted, thus undercutting the very centrism he so loudly proclaimed. It was dubbed the *Koinonia Statement.*

A confidential letter he wrote to a bishop in 1997 as Bishop of Chicago, revealed that he had no problem with active, non-celibate homosexuals, acting out their sexuality as priests in The Episcopal Church.

Presiding Bishop Griswold and the evangelical Archbishop of Canterbury, George Carey, fought repeatedly over the universal truth of the gospel message. Carey attempted to dialogue with Griswold concerning his massive social agenda. Carey writes, "It seemed to me that he and others sympathetic to this trend were ignoring the catholicity of truth."

Carey noted that churches such as Roman Catholic, Baptist and non-denominational churches were more willing to be distinctive. One reason the Episcopal Church is declining, is that it is "more likely to modify faith claims in the cause of liberal conformity to culture," Carey wrote.

"On reflection I had a distinct impression that the Episcopal Church had been infiltrated by its culture more profoundly than its leaders and members realized. Instead of sustaining a creative spiritual and intellectual critique of culture, the Church was inclined to accept the prevailing therapeutic 'feel-goodism' and pragmatic indices of success as gifts of the Spirit. While some adaptation to culture has to happen in order for mission to be successful, to be relevant culturally also means being different—otherwise 'conversion', 'repentance', and 'forgiveness' have lost their meaning," Carey opined.

Griswold didn't care about the universal truth of the Christian faith. In truth, he had abandoned it.

The more Carey tried to communicate with Griswold, the more Griswold cut him off.

Carey noted that everywhere he went while visiting the Episcopal Church in the United States, the issue was about practicing homosexual priests. "I was taken aback by the way this matter was raised in my presence again and again. It was not on my agenda as an issue, but whether I liked it or not I was challenged to explain my position and substantiate my opposition to practicing homosexuality."

Carey made a number of strong conclusions. "If the Episcopal Church of the United States has tended to be seduced by the prevailing culture of its society, with no overarching strategy for discerning where the lines should be drawn, my visit to some African countries revealed that other provinces were consciously, and often unconsciously, struggling to work out the implications of the Christian faith in cultures that were not entirely inimical to it."

Carey repeatedly asked the Episcopal Church to grow into counter-cultural relationship with the zeitgeist. Carey described the problems of the American House of Bishops that he saw during his visit in 1992.

"Beneath the friendliness and courtesy of the way the Americans worked, it became clear to me that there were deep divisions. A small but significant number of Bishops were disenfranchised from the rest. Some felt alienated because they were traditional Catholics who, because they opposed the ordination of women, believed that they were being forced out of the Church. Others felt estranged from the House of Bishops because they challenged the strong liberal agenda that prevailed there. It saddened me that there did not appear to be an overarching unity that held them together."

Carey attempted to begin a dialogue about these differences, but Griswold did not respond to his invitation to dialogue. Instead, he charged ahead with plans to consecrate an active homosexual to the episcopate.

The Robinson-Griswold Confrontation with The Anglican Communion

In the 1970s, the future Bishop Gene Robinson, was ascending rapidly up through the ranks of the Episcopal Church. Born in Kentucky in 1947, Robinson, in an interview, describes his early years. "I had grown up in the church. I never knew what it was like not to be in the church." He talks about his earliest religious experience. "I grew up in a very small, rural, poor church, the Disciples of Christ denomination, so I come out of a very evangelical background. We had a two-week tent revival meeting every summer, and it was during one of those that I gave my life to Christ. I was twelve or thirteen years old; I believe."

Also, Robinson started having sexual relations with men. He says that he went into therapy to enable himself to have a relationship with a woman and married following this.

Robinson went to the Episcopal seminary at Sewanee University of the South and, while there, he said he had a pivotal spiritual experience at a Little Brothers of Jesus community.

Yet, even after coming out as a homosexual, Robinson faced the sadness of changing his life around to allow for his coming out. He discussed the difficulties of the end of his marriage.

"I was married for thirteen years, and I and my wife "Boo" struggled with it till the end." Robinson said he feared coming out as gay, but then was delighted to discover that the Episcopal Church, instead of turning away from him, actually promoted him.

The stage was completely set for the confrontation with the Anglican Communion. Archbishop George Carey had traveled throughout the United States trying to dialogue, but all he received was criticism.

Carey took a strong stand against the blessing of same sex unions.

"In the case of same sex relationships, I think it would be a grievous error to offer some sort of 'blessing' that is a pretended substitute for a marriage, which such a union can never comprise. To do this is to harm the people involved by offering them a pretense and a deception. To borrow a telling American phrase, it is an 'act of pastoral violence.' But to perform such an act is also to mislead society at large. Offering such ceremonies seems to suggest that something resembling a marriage can exist where it does not. It is also a trivialization of gender. If a shop pretends to sell goods and services it cannot in fact provide, we all know this to be wrong—and the Church is in this respect no different." (298-299)

Carey's use of the phrase "act of pastoral violence" is a reference to an article by Bishop Spong, who writes, "A well-known national pastoral counseling agency called any effort to change a person's sexual orientation 'an act of pastoral violence.'" Spong did not name this national agency.

Because of the stand he took, Carey received and experienced grave criticism from opposing groups. Carey described the press statement of the Lesbian and Gay Christian Movement in which he was called "'heartless,' 'cruel,' a 'bigot' and 'homophobic.'"(307) Carey deplored that language and said it stopped any meaningful dialogue.

Carey repeatedly urged the Episcopal Church to adopt a counter-cultural position to its surrounding society. Carey took a strong stand against the move towards the blessing of same-sex unions as well as the ordination of homosexuals and lesbians. He paid a price for this both in lagging popularity in the United States and criticism for his refusal to change. Carey based his belief against the blessing of same sex unions on scripture, especially in Romans 1: 26-28. Carey found the witness of Paul's letter compelling and said that the Anglican Communion must listen to the scriptural truth found in Paul's Letter to Romans.

In December 2002, Rowan Williams was elected the 104th Archbishop of Canterbury and his office quickly became inundated with the besetting problems in the US Episcopal Church.

Plans to Consecrate Gene Robinson

On June 7, 2003, the Episcopal Church's Diocese of New Hampshire elected Gene Robinson as its new diocesan bishop.

Williams called a summit in London in October 2003, after many Anglicans objected to the plans to confirm the Rev. V. Gene Robinson as bishop-elect for the Diocese of New Hampshire. The U.S. and Canadian churches had already permitted the blessing of same-sex unions.

"If [Robinson's] consecration proceeds, we recognize that we have reached a crucial and critical point in the life of the Anglican Communion, and we have had to conclude that the future of the Communion itself will be put in jeopardy," the statement said.

In London, Griswold called the discussions "difficult but truthful" and told reporters he had no intention of asking Robinson to step down, although anything could happen between now and then, he said.

"The Second Coming could occur, which would certainly cancel the whole thing," he said sarcastically.

The primates also asked provinces to find a way to provide pastoral care to parishes that are uncomfortable with the views expressed by their bishops, perhaps by allowing visiting bishops to minister to them.

Griswold was viewed by the Global South as a moral compromiser and doctrinally fluid leader of a rapidly diminishing church that was busy bludgeoning its orthodox wing into the ground by his gang of blitzkrieg revisionist bishops.

The Consecration of Gene Robinson

It became clear now why Griswold felt he could proceed with the consecration of Gene Robinson. They had both traveled far, far away from the Christian faith and left Jesus Christ far behind. That tent revival faith of Gene Robinson's had been swallowed up and destroyed by his homoeroticism and the need for personal self-validation.

At the Robinson consecration service, some still tried to stop it with confrontational action. The protests were mild and orderly.

The Rev. Dr. Earle Fox tried to explain some of the actual sexual activities that went on between homosexuals, but Griswold cut him off, "I plead you, spare us these details and come to the substance, please."

"You know where I am headed? Then I have made my point?" At this point, Fr. Fox left the stand.

The second protest was from a woman from Robinson's New Hampshire diocese, who warned, "If this consecration goes forward, the Anglican fabric will be torn."

The Rt. Rev. David Bena offered the third protest in the form of a letter signed by thirty-six United States and Canadian bishops who refused to recognize Robinson's consecration. Bishop David Bena read, "This consecration poses a dramatic contradiction to the historic faith and discipline of the church. We join with the majority of bishops in the Anglican Communion and will not recognize it."

With the protests ended, the ceremony proceeded. Robinson knelt down, while a crowd of bishops vested in traditional red robes surrounded him. Then Presiding Bishop, Frank Griswold, prayed, "Make Gene a bishop in your church. Pour out upon him the power of your princely Spirit, whom you bestowed upon your beloved Son Jesus Christ, with whom he endowed the apostles, and by whom your Church is built up in every place, to the glory and unceasing praise of your Name." Hands of bishops reached out to touch Gene's head to affirm his succession in the Christian apostles since the time of St. Peter.

When Gene arose following his consecration, a new day had begun in Christian history. For the first time, a declared homosexual man with a male partner had been consecrated bishop.

Following the consecration, the global fallout was unprecedented. The Archbishop of Canterbury, Rowan Williams, warned that the consecration had "very serious consequences for the cohesion of the Anglican Communion."

The continuing loss of members and financial resources concerned many and started to accelerate. In 1965, The Episcopal Church had 3.5 million; it would drop by half over the next decade. Both the American Anglican Council and the Episcopal Church released information that the Episcopal Church dropped in 2002 by 8,209 members, but in 2003 and 2004, membership declined by 35,988 and 36,414 respectively to a total of over two million members. Episcopal leaders had to finally acknowledge their declining membership.

Robinson had appeared to have a perfect marriage as a heterosexual. It was a lie. He appeared to have a perfect marriage as a homosexual. It, too, was a lie. Both ended in divorce. Then it emerged that Robinson was an alcoholic. When challenged, Robinson opined that this was a "private matter."

Robinson's life was all over the map and he cursed the entire Anglican Communion for its homophobia, never looking back to see the destruction he had wrought and the universal damage he had done to the whole Communion.

And this is the man Frank Griswold consecrated as the Ninth Bishop of New Hampshire!

Two bishops, John W. Howe (Central Florida) and William Wantland (Eau Claire), both wrote letters telling Griswold to resign for his consecration of V. Gene Robinson, but their pleas went ignored.

Howe ripped Griswold in a letter saying he had ignored the counsel of the Archbishop of Canterbury, the Meeting of the Anglican Primates, the Anglican Communion Council, the most recent Lambeth Conference (in 1998), and the Theology Committee of the House of Bishops.

"You have ignored the clear teaching of scripture, 5,000 years of Judeo-Christian tradition, the last seven General Conventions of the Episcopal Church (prior to this summer's 74th General Convention), the pleas of Primates and Provinces of the Anglican Communion from around the world, and those of our ecumenical partners, including the Holy Father in Rome, and the Conventions of (at least) six of our dioceses. We have ordained and consecrated, as a bishop in the Church of God, a non-celibate homosexual man, openly living in a "partnered" relationship with another man for the past thirteen years. We have thus repudiated the promise of the House of Bishops' Study Document of 1994, to ordain "only persons we believe to be a wholesome example to their people, according to the standards and norms set forth by the Church's teaching [which is] that...the standard found in the New Testament of lifelong, monogamous, heterosexual union as the setting intended by God for sexual relationships between men and women is the foundation on which the Church's traditional teaching is built."

"We have violated the commitment made in that same Study Document to commit to ongoing consultation concerning these matters with the wider Anglican Communion and with our ecumenical partners before proceeding with such innovations."

"We have betrayed tens of thousands loyal Episcopalians, bewildered the Christian world, and grieved the Holy Spirit."

Howe concluded his blast by saying Griswold and his fellow revisionist bishops should resign their positions in the Episcopal Church, USA.

The Aftermath of Griswold's Consecration of Robinson

Seven lean years into his episcopacy, Frank Griswold had united nobody and nothing, and his promise to be a presiding bishop for all was hysterically laughable, if it wasn't so damnably tragic.

In 2004, The Episcopal Church stood on the edge of being publicly reprimanded, if not thrown out of the Anglican Communion for doctrinal and moral infidelity, with Griswold himself personally shunned by the vast majority of African, Asian and Southern Cone Primates.

Within the Episcopal Church, at least three movements sprang up to challenge the revisionist steam-roller led by Griswold - The American Anglican Council, The Network (NADCP) and the Anglican Communion Institute. A fourth movement, Forward in Faith, the traditionalist wing of the ECUSA, was reinvigorated for the battle with two priests at that time ready to be consecrated bishops.

Because of his actions, Griswold was forced to resign as Episcopal co-chair of the Anglican–Roman Catholic International Commission Dialogue Committee (ARCIC) talks for his pro homosexual position. He was publicly rebuked by the Russian Orthodox Church and was told that he was not welcome on the African continent by most of the Anglican Communion's African Primates.

The Rt. Rev. Michael Nazir-Ali, then Bishop of Rochester who served with Griswold noted that right after the Gene Robinson consecration, the RC co-chair refused to co-chair with him and another chair had to be found.

He was specifically uninvited to the consecration of the new Ugandan Primate, Henry Orombi, and he was publicly blasted for his actions in consecrating an openly homoerotic bishop, by the Primate of the largest province in the communion, Peter Akinola of Nigeria. "It's Satanic," said the Council of Anglican Provinces of Africa (CAPA) leader.

He lied when he told the Nigerians he was an Anglo-Catholic, when, in fact, he is closer to being an Affirming Catholic, though some theologians dispute even that, saying that his views are closer to "mystic paganism" and his constant mention of Sufi Rumi makes him a universalist and pantheist.

If Griswold had been the head of an American corporation, he would have been forced to resign, publicly humiliated for his theological and moral positions and for his blatant disregard for the 'faith once for all delivered to the saints', turning his back on the very faith he swore to uphold and defend.

There had never been a leader of any branch of the Anglican Communion in modern history, so blatantly apostate and heretical, who lived and worked for the overthrow of the very things he said he would support and sustain than Frank Griswold.

He put at risk whole branches of the communion for his pro-Islamic statements, and his public affirmation of pansexuality jeopardized the lives of Anglicans in Northern Nigeria, who daily face the onslaughts of Islamic fundamentalists pushing Sharia law, who laughingly mock Christianity as a 'queer' religion.

African Primates could only stand in mute silence against such public onslaughts of their faith, knowing that what happens in the American Episcopal Church and the Anglican Church of Canada affects them in their countries.

Griswold's spiritual hero, if not his mentor, became the famous 13th century Sufi poet, Rumi, whom he quoted freely when caught in situations that demanded an absolute response. When Fr. David Moyer, a traditionalist priest on Philadelphia's Main Line, appealed to him to intervene in his battle with revisionist Pennsylvania Bishop, Charles Bennison, Griswold said, "I think here of the words of the Sufi poet Rumi: 'Beyond ideas of wrongdoing and rightdoing there lies a field. I'll meet you there. It is my fervent hope that some modality can be found acceptable both to you and the Church of the Good Shepherd that will allow you to meet in that field'."

In truth, Griswold was powerless to resolve their dispute because they had mutually contradictory positions that could not be reconciled. To find that point of reconciliation, Griswold would have had to admit that Bennison's actions were wrong and Moyer's right. So deeply conflicted was Griswold about the issues, that to find a "solution" he wandered off into a spiritual no man's land. By doing nothing, he revealed a spinelessness that has followed him throughout his tenure.

Theologian Robert Sanders correctly diagnosed Griswold's thinking and theology as little more than "mystic paganism".

Griswold made multiple charges including adultery against former New York bishop, Richard Grein, disappear, even as he excoriated the actions of faithful bishops who intervened on behalf of faithful parishes in revisionist dioceses.

He managed to keep his job because a majority of some 61 bishops in the House of Bishops believed and thought as he did and shared his bankrupt theological outlook.

While he claimed to speak for the "diverse center", it was increasingly apparent that such a center no longer existed, and that the church was rapidly polarizing around right and wrong, truth and lies, good and evil.

He frantically crossed the ocean to schmooze former Archbishop of Canterbury, George Carey into making him think that the Anglican Mission in America was the Evil Empire in the midst of ECUSA, when all they were trying to do was uphold the faith that he, Griswold, should have been doing all along.

He hung on for dear life to Dr. Rowan Williams, even as he blew off his fellow primates, saying that he did not really care what they thought as long as Williams continued to recognize him.

Griswold's tenure as presiding bishop was marked by betrayal, betrayal of trust and his actions have been called schismatic. He had zero commitment to the authority of Holy Scripture and his actions in the House of Bishops have been called by one bishop "manipulative and duplicitous."

His "pluriform" theology and views only isolated the orthodox branches of his church and the consecration of Robinson as a "new thing God is doing" was, in fact, a contradiction of what God actually said!

Griswold had no intention of stopping or repealing his church's drive towards full pansexual acceptance. On *National Public Radio*, Griswold made himself perfectly clear again by "contextualizing" the debate. He said that homosexuality was not unique to the US and Canada, adding that the issue was really a cultural one, avoiding any mention of what the Bible said, and deflecting a statement by Rowan Williams, who said that ECUSA's "actions have fractured the Communion." Williams understood that the Anglican Communion could be fractured by Robinson's consecration and he worked desperately to keep this branch of the Christian faith together. Williams went on to say that someone is going to have to say "Yes, we were wrong." Not Frank Tracy Griswold.

Griswold's sermons too, became homilies of ambiguity and obfuscation, capable of multiple interpretations. A one-time rector of Grace Church, Massachusetts, said of Griswold's sermons that it was like walking through a horse stable and being reminded not to step on a Griswold.

Bishop Griswold became the embodiment of his own pluriform thinking. Tragically, the Pluriform One has been diminished by his making it, and, as one thoughtful observer noted, he has by doing so, become the least authentic bishop alive, the late mover, tester of responses, submissive to the discipline of consent.

Typical of Griswold are statements he would make that, when taken at face value, were contradictory and shallow. When called upon to answer his critics, Griswold fudged his response, blaming one newspaper, the *Boston Globe*, for misquoting him.

"An honest man would either affirm or deny the quote from the *Globe*, but he (Griswold) does neither," said one commentator.

A classic example was Griswold being quoted as saying: "Please pray that the spirit of truth will carry us beyond the realm of logic and of agreement and disagreement into that deeper place of love."

The Rev. Dr. Earle Fox, an orthodox Episcopal apologist, said that it verifies the charge that he (Griswold) has left the Christian faith. "One cannot believe truth to be relative, or essentially ambiguous, one cannot reject the law of non-contradiction, and remain a Biblical believer. It is nonsense to talk of a place beyond logic and beyond agreement and disagreement. (What else could the word 'nonsense' mean if not 'in violation of the laws of logic and of fact"?) No one can act that way, including Griswold. It is precisely our personal, relating, acting nature which forces us to be logical. The law of God is not meant to be ambiguous, any more than any other law. Laws are about enforcement, which is one-way, either/or, not both/and."

Fox went further, saying Griswold might make a good Hindu or Gnostic, but he is not a Christian, not in his teaching and behavior. "He cannot say that he is faithful to Christ. The very claim is meaningful only if it has logical and factual consistency."

A statement Griswold made to the *Boston Globe* stating that a large body of scientific evidence had concluded that sexual orientation is innate, got him into hot water with a Christian apologist, a bishop and a psychiatrist.

"You were represented as saying that there was a large body of evidence supporting the notion that homosexuality was innate, when in fact no such body of evidence exists," they wrote to Griswold.

When told that the public relations campaign by homosexual activists in recent years had convinced many Christians to believe in scientific evidence that, in fact, did not exist and that such false information placed millions of people at increased risk for moral and spiritual compromise as well as for major disease and significantly shortened life span, Griswold responded; "Suffice it to say that the article in the newspaper report to which you refer was an interpretation of my views emerging in a long interview. I said that the biblical passages about sexuality must be looked at from the context of what was known about human sexuality at the time of their writing. Our understanding of the complexities of the human mind and body has grown enormously over these centuries. We have learned much from science about the origins of sexuality, and I venture there is more to be discovered."

Griswold capped his remarks saying that the contemporary understanding of human sexuality is much more advanced than it was in Biblical times. "A large body of scientific evidence has concluded that sexual orientation is innate, not chosen. Scripture has to be put in its own historical, social context."

In an interview with the *Trinity Journal for Theology and Ministry,* in the fall of 2008, Griswold said, "St. Paul very clearly assumed that everyone was, by nature, heterosexual. Therefore, in Paul's time, homosexuality was a willing choice made by the wicked against God's natural order. Our current understanding, has been altered by God's unfolding revelation of truth."

In his travels to dioceses around the country, Griswold opined about how impressed he was by "how healthy the church is, how very much alive it is, and how much is going on in ministry and in witness." But the truth is Griswold saw what he wanted to see, and refused to acknowledge the deep, underlying fissures that were beginning to open before his very eyes. Over time, almost every diocese had dissenting parishes, and litigation costs mounted daily as revisionist bishops fought orthodox parish priests for their properties. Griswold's "gospel" was coming home to roost.

Griswold repeatedly called on Episcopalians to listen to each other, but he never truly listened to the orthodox with a sufficiently compassionate heart to respond to their concerns. Listening was always one-sided, in the end when confronted by the obvious contradiction that homosexual practice could not be reconciled with biblical revelation, he resorted to "justice" as a means to impress those of orthodox persuasion. That, too, failed.

Griswold's out and out support of homosexuality only deepened the widening rift in the ECUSA and he acknowledged the seriousness of the debate, saying he understood why passions run so high on both sides of the issue. "Those who believe that gays and lesbians should be ordained and have their relationships blessed by the church believe the gifts of the spirit are present in the lives of many homosexuals."

But is dying early a gift of the Spirit? Is a compulsive and lethal behavior a gift of the Spirit? Is massive promiscuity and being obsessed with sex a gift of the Spirit? Just where is this gift of the Spirit and what does it have to do with being in this chaos?

The sylph-like Griswold danced ballet-like around difficult issues, ineptly dodging an undodgeable bullet by changing the subject and blaming the media, for what he said and for exposing his shameless "truths". It became commonplace, almost comical, to hear his repeated attacks on certain unnamed Internet writers disseminating falsehoods about The Episcopal Church.

Griswold was constantly reminded by orthodox laity, bishops and primates of the need to repent of his sins, not explain them away. "We call Frank Griswold to stand up, be the spiritual leader for the rest of us which Christ is calling him to be, and to publicly repent of his evasion of truth in this life and death matter of sexuality," wrote three leaders.

For nearly a decade, Griswold lived with the Episcopal Church's ambiguity and bipolar vision in theology and morals, neither condemning Spong's Unitarian 12 Theses, nor forbidding sexual relations outside of heterosexual marriage. His positions only hardened throughout his tenure as presiding bishop.

A close friend, who has known Griswold for most of his ecclesiastical career, described him as having a sort of "Zen spirituality", a tumbler of one-part Anglo-Catholicism with one-part Eastern mysticism, laced with a liberal splash of post modernism, topped off with a twist of pluralism.

The Presiding Bishop has, in turn, dallied with the Dalai Lama, prostrated himself before the Moscow Patriarchate, pressed the flesh with the Pope, mingled with Anglican Primates, and, when it was finally made public (what many of us already knew) that his church was in theological shambles with 'irregular' consecrations, he dashed across the pond to be embraced by Archbishop George Carey and affirmed in his position as putative head of the American Episcopal Church.

Frank Griswold saw no contradiction in any of this. He gave off an air of almost waif-like charm, so charming in fact that even his detractors, that is, those bishops who profoundly disagreed with him about his stands on human sexuality, found him nonetheless strangely appealing, exuding an air of mystic-like spirituality that was at once both compelling and ethereal. There was an unmistakable feminine sensuality to the man when you met him in person. True to form, he abstained from voting on the Lambeth sexuality 1.10 resolution. A tight-rope walker to the end.

Griswold's Reputation and Sexuality

His own sexuality was the private talk of many. Was he really masquerading as a bi-sexual? In 2006, VOL wrote a story about his consorting with homosexuals in Paris when he was Bishop of Chicago.

An Episcopal bishop told me that Griswold consorted with known drag queens and homosexuals in Paris in the late 80's.

The bishop said he was finally glad to tell someone the truth about Griswold, as he had watched with dismay the decline of The Episcopal Church under his tenure.

The bishop said Griswold would come with his wife Phoebe to Paris, and then disappear into the Left Bank, leaving her with the wife of the American Bishop of Europe.

"Griswold told me he wanted to preach sermons at the cathedral. I let him preach once and it was terrible. I said he could never preach again. The next Sunday he turned up with a bunch of bad looking people, dressed in odd clothes with heavy black make-up around their eyes and I told him not to bring those people from the other side of the river into my cathedral."

Griswold never returned.

"I didn't trust Griswold at all. I said to my Dean 'keep that friend of yours away from the cathedral.' The dean replied, "He's not my friend." He said he thought we had to have him preach because he was a bishop. The cathedral bishop said he had no respect for Griswold, "and neither did my Dean."

The retired bishop then said he relayed the whole scene to an orthodox American bishop when he returned to the U.S., who spoke to VirtueOnline and confirmed what the American bishop had told him.

Asked what his overall impression of Griswold was, the bishop said his impression was that Griswold was a sort of sissy. "I was very surprised he became Presiding Bishop. John Allin [former Presiding Bishop] told me he didn't like him. My memory of him is that he was a weak man.'

There were allegations that Griswold had assignations with men at a Gramercy Park apartment block owned by the Episcopal Parish of Calvary-St. George's in New York City.

He is an enigma some say that has no resolution in this life. He dances, pan-like around issues. Jack Spong, in his book "*Here I Stand*" says of Griswold that he lacked "commitment and courage" for his stands, waffling on issues that, to Spong's mind, showed Griswold lacking in character. Spong, who has never been afraid to say what he did and did not believe, had no use for Griswold, who couched things in a way as to leave you wondering what he really meant and where he stood on an issue.

A case in point was the Primates' meeting in Oporto, which unambiguously called for a reaffirmation of the Lambeth statement on human sexuality, calling the American Episcopal Church to a stricter accountability on sexuality, proscribing same-sex marriages and homosexual behavior. Returning to America and questioned on how this would translate to the Church here, Griswold said, "We have moved into a deeper place...a place of far more costly and authentic communion."

What did that mean? What deeper place, where was it? What's the roadmap for finding it? No one dared ask, no one truly knows. His answer bore no relation to the question. His answers rarely did. Griswold plunged into a faux mysticism to explain the ambiguity in himself, not in what he hears from his fellow Primates. It is the language of obfuscation that Griswold seems comfortable espousing. He lives on the frontlines of linguistic ambiguity, hedging his answers in ways that resemble the mystic rather than the rationalist. He is at once both thoroughly post-modern and strangely mystical at the same time.

When the former president of Trinity Episcopal School for Ministry, Dr. Peter Moore, delivered a paper to 1,000 Evangelical Episcopalians in Ridgecrest, NC, he said pluralism and post-modernism go hand in hand. Frank Griswold imbibes both, moving comfortably between the two like a man carrying two drinks from which he sips simultaneously, testing each for viscosity and flavor.

When he was bishop of Chicago, Bishop Frank Griswold is quoted as having said that limiting salvation exclusively to Christ is "Jesusolatry." It is a perfect Griswold line. Of course, Jesus is the way, but not the only way, what are we say of all the other religions in the world? Christians are a mere two billion in a world of six billion. A Christless eternity is unthinkable. God loves all and saves all, anything less would make God bad and unloving and that would never do.

Griswold's Chicago Diocese

The November/December 1993 edition of *Anglican Advance,* the official news publication of the Diocese of Chicago, reported that in the thirty years prior to the 2003 consecration of Gene Robinson as the first openly gay bishop in the Anglican Communion, the Rt. Rev.

James Montgomery, during his 25-year tenure, secretly encouraged many closeted gay clergy to come to Chicago, where they could be ordained and licensed with no questions asked. The diocese gave cover in November, 1974, for Louie Crew and two other homosexual men from Chicago to form Integrity, a pro-gay activist group that began working immediately for the full inclusion of gays and lesbians in the Episcopal Church. The movement spread rapidly from its Chicago epicenter.

Bishop Montgomery was succeeded in 1987 by Bishop Frank Griswold who continued Montgomery's policy of welcoming and ordaining actively homosexual clergy in the Diocese of Chicago. The new Bishop of Chicago also initiated other changes, such as establishing a tacit, open communion policy at St. James Cathedral, allowing all present to receive communion whether or not they were baptized Christians. At the same time, a small parish in West Chicago, Church of the Resurrection, began a healing service on Wednesday evenings, which included ministry to persons beset by sexual brokenness, including those experiencing unwanted same sex attraction.

By 1993, it became clear that Griswold and the Church of the Resurrection were at odds. The bishop stated that he believed it "quite possible for a homosexual person not committed to celibacy to live a wholesome and profoundly Christian life." The Resurrection clergy and vestry held fast to the Biblical teaching on sexual morality and through their ministry, people experiencing same-sex attraction, began to receive profound healing and restoration to wholeness. Things came to a head when a young man from Resurrection entered the diocesan discernment process for holy orders and was informed by Griswold that he need not remain celibate as ordained clergy if he found himself attracted to other men. Ongoing conversations between Griswold and the Resurrection's clergy revealed that the differences between them were irreconcilable and that the bishop was actively undermining Resurrection's Scriptural teaching and ministry. On October 30, Resurrection's vestry voted unanimously to disassociate from the Diocese of Chicago. Griswold then unilaterally deposed Resurrection's clergy for "renunciation of orders" and the congregation decided to walk away from its property rather than fight the diocese.

What Uganda Archbishop, Stanley Ntagali, would later call "a spiritual cancer" had already been well-established in the Diocese of Chicago and other liberal TEC parishes some twenty years earlier.

When Griswold was asked in 1997, how he planned to grow the church, he openly admitted that he didn't have a clue. It would happen, he thought, when people came to realize the beauty of the Episcopal tradition, its historic record, its openness to the world, its inclusivity. It never happened, of course. The church has slowly, and latterly been emptying at a breathtaking pace.

Griswold deflects anger at him by consulting a psychiatrist, reading the Psalms, and going deeper into his mystical self, where all language and lines are blurred. But his is not the mysticism of the Desert Fathers or St. John of the Cross, of a Berdyaev or Dostoevsky.

In fact, as you read his speeches and sermons, certain words appear with monotonous regularity. Words like 'dialogue', 'diversity', 'openness', 'nonjudgmental', 'fractal harmony', 'inclusive' and, above all, 'tolerance'. His only absolute is that there are no absolutes.

In Frank Griswold's mind, the life of the Church should be marked by fluidity and openness in morals and theology. Whatever you do, never say you "know" something is absolutely true, it might rule out a truth somewhere else that might call into question the very truth you believe in. You are free to choose, but never choose too dogmatically; you might have to change that choice. Always be open to the winds of change or winds of the spirit, wherever they might lead.

Take for example, another statement of Griswold's regarding his discreet endorsement of the United Religions Initiative much ballyhooed by Bishop William E. Swing of California (where else, pray tell, in a state that will see 500 new religions like IPOs spring up this year.)

Of this movement, Bishop Griswold noted his gratefulness to the first bishop of California, and said that "determined farsightedness is a characteristic I particularly associate with this diocese and many of its bishops across the years...as well as your present bishop's vision of the potential force of the world's religions to bind up and bring together, rather than divide and turn the people of the earth against one another."

It is not the cross that people should turn to for faith and repentance that Griswold appeals to "to bind up the broken-hearted" or bring "release to the captives", it is religion, all religions that pose a powerful force for unity on earth. Griswold hated Mel Gibson's movie *The Passion of the Christ,* it was too violent and bloody. Griswold could not stomach the notion of substitutionary atonement, nail pierced hands, a sweating God dripping blood. It offended his sensitive persona and his view of a more milquetoast God, loving and embracing all.

Like many who crave peace and unity, Griswold sees the events of history not in linear terms culminating in "...Christ will come again" but in the repetition of cycles wherein Man will move forward and upward away from his darker self. It is not in the way of the cross, but in human initiatives for peace on earth that Griswold yearns.

The Episcopal Church's current understanding of mission is not the call of The Great Commission, but the call for people of good will along with United Nations mandates and resolutions calling for peace on earth without bending the knee to the Prince of Peace.

The demons Griswold hated are, of course, "fundamentalists" - Christian, Moslem, Hindu, but especially Christian and those who may lurk in the bosom of ECUSA. Griswold reveals his "absolute" in those moments of outburst and frustration. For it is in those statements that Griswold's pluriformity crashes and burns. His violent outburst in the HOB reveals only the tip of his melting pluralist iceberg.

Griswold cannot face "absolute" evil. As the Twin Towers came crashing to the ground, courtesy of fanatical Islamists on that fateful 9/11, Griswold blamed American foreign policy and Western Islamophobia, not Al Qaeda. He could not look evil in the face and name it.

At the end, Frank Tracy Griswold is the true universalist in thought, word and deed, eschewing anything that smells of particularity or exclusivity. Griswold demonstrate the open heart, the open mind, the transgendered body, ever seeking but never coming to a knowledge of the truth. For Frank Griswold, there is no absolute truth, and therein lies his hell.

One bishop had the audacity to ask Griswold how he could hold all of these "pluriform truths" together in his mind.

The truth is, he doesn't. Anything and everything are now acceptable to Griswold except orthodoxy, for the orthodox are the only remnant left standing in his way for a complete makeover of the church, even as it heads in Gadarene fashion towards the ecclesiastical cliff.

Bishop Wantland wrote, following the Robinson consecration, "This is not only necessary for the Church, but for your own spiritual well-being. You have betrayed the Christian Faith. In the words of our baptismal liturgy, you need to 'repent and return to the Lord'."

"You have rejected the Faith," wrote the traditionalist bishop, "but [I hope] that this separation might bring you back to the truth." It never did.

Griswold's signature on the *Koininia Statement* that Spong wrote and that Browning also supported, cemented Griswold firmly in the homosexual camp. It raised many questions in a number of quarters about his own sexuality. Was he covering his own narcissistic bisexuality by embracing pansexuality?

Challenged, he has said he would never "betray homosexuals" in the Church by unsigning his name from Spong's *Koinonia* statement. He was also very comfortable around homosexuals like V. Gene Robinson and Louie Crew, and the church's national headquarters was filled with homosexuals and lesbians at all levels. He also refused to draw back or reprimand dioceses that had resolved to include transgendered and lesbitransgay behavior. He decried absolutist theological positions. It was the only absolute, apart from tolerance that he held sacred.

Amidst it all, he took time out to slip into jeans and go off to Mass and take Holy Communion at a Roman Catholic Church in New York City, even though that violated Catholic teaching.

Griswold was about the agenda he was promoting and conditioning the Church to accept. He evoked spiritual ideas and auras and used language like nobody else had ever done.

Griswold used language in a similar way to that of Spong, but much more mystically. It was humanistic and all about feelings, dripping with sentiment and lots of gooey stuff. Here is an example:

On January 10, 1999, Griswold preached a sermon at the Washington National Cathedral. Talking about the role of presiding bishop he says that he should minister to other households of faith as well. As sign, symbol, and instrument, the Presiding Bishop must always seek the larger view, the broader perspective that embraces and includes, and call the community to seek the Truth who is Christ in one another, and in the diversity of our responses to the rigors of the gospel and the leading of the Holy Spirit.

It was grandiose, narcissistic thinking. What in the world was he talking about? The Presiding Bishop is a sign, symbol and instrument…? No, he was supposed to uphold the faith and be a faithful Christian committed to the gospel of Christ.

So, what did Griswold care about?

He cared about Islamic Sufism and 13th century poetry by one particular Sufi, Rumi. He writes about it at length in his book *Going Home: An Invitation to Jubilee.* In this section, Griswold dodges the word Islamic and uses the term Sufi (one of the three forms of Islam) over and over again. Griswold also failed to footnote his source with a page number.

Here is the poem his words spill out about.

Out beyond ideas of wrongdoing and rightdoing,

there is a field. I'll meet you there.

When the soul lies down in that grass,

the world is too full to talk about.

Ideas, language, even the phrase "each other" doesn't make any sense.

mevlana jelaluddin rumi - 13th century

Griswold loved this stuff to the point of embarrassing his hearers and readers.

"Are we ready to make the journey to that field?" Griswold gushed.

Griswold was the melted chocolate flowing onto the Rumi's strawberry. Griswold was the outer decoration, Rumi the substance. Both Rumi and Griswold seemed to be describing the loss of the Way.

Griswold went beyond right and wrong and beyond the Christian faith and its Hebrew tradition.

Sufi Rumi equaled Griswold's consciousness.

Griswold lost the focus of a personal God. He destroyed the resurrected and transcendent Lord Christ and berated those who needed an exclusionary faith. Griswold took a subjective feeling of something, called it 'Beloved,' like the Islamic Sufis did.

Griswold was so enamored by the Sufi world he had embraced he asked the House of Bishops to dance what he called the *Circle Dance of Dispossession*, in lieu of the need to confess sin. He used the term Christ consciousness, to invoke a highly human developed consciousness, thus rejecting any idea of our truth that Jesus is Lord and Savior of the world.

Though a Harvard educated English major, he forgets — or decides not to — attribute the sources of his ideas and quotes.

Griswold has at least 20 quotes in his book and he footnotes only one of them correctly. Any high school student today knows how to attribute sources.

Griswold's exploration of taking faithful Episcopalians into Islamic beliefs was neither incidental nor accidental. He realized that the church was dying and he wanted to pave the way for subsequent presiding bishops who would follow his plan.

Browning cleared the stage by moving the Christian faith out, while Griswold moved Islamic and New Age mysticism in - front and center stage.

The Saga of Bishop Otis Charles

An example of something that happened under Griswold revealed Griswold's thinking.

Bishop Otis Charles presided as Bishop of Utah from 1971-1985, and later became Dean of the Episcopal Divinity School in Massachusetts from 1985-1993. After his retirement, Charles became the first Episcopal bishop to come out of the closet and declare he was homosexual. That was in 1993. He was now 63, had divorced his wife of 42 years and left her to move to San Francisco.

According to an interview with the San Francisco Chronicle on April 29, 2004, Charles began to date men while he adjusted to his new life-style. He eventually fell in love with his future male partner, Felipe Sanchez Paris. The announcement went out that Charles would have an Episcopal ceremony called a "consecration of their life together" in San Francisco. His new partner, Felipe, had four ex-wives, while the bishop had been previously married to one woman.

During the ceremony, Charles wore his bishop's purple shirt. The wedding ceremony ended with the bishop and his new spouse presiding in throne-like chairs and being paraded around the streets of San Francisco.

Did Griswold see this as the growing 'Christ consciousness' of Charles and was he secretly happy that some Episcopalians were going beyond right and wrong, honoring marriage vows? Including their wives, a group of seven people had gone beyond thinking that those confining marriage vows were to be honored. Did all of those rejected women agree that divorce would increase personal wholeness and well-being and multidimensional thinking in their lives?

What had Charles taught in seminary to future ordinands? What of Jesus' teaching that we enter through the narrow gate, for wide is the gate and broad is the road that leads to destruction, and many enter through it. (Matthew 7:13.)

In his book, Griswold gushes, "Love shatters our defenses and opens us to surprise and possibility beyond our wildest imagining." (pg. 41).

Global South primates lodged strong protests against the Episcopal Church. At Dromantine, in Northern Ireland, in February 2005, the Primates issued a closing communiqué that upheld the Communion's traditional teaching on Scriptural authority and human sexuality. A dozen Anglican leaders, mostly from Africa, refused to take communion with Presiding Bishop Frank T. Griswold.

Griswold finally got the message; the Global South primates would not back his efforts to legitimize homosexual relationships, prompting Griswold to respond that he discerned "the father of lies and the devil" moving about Dromantine, aka orthodox Primates like Nigerian primate Peter Akinola et al.

Before he departed Dromantine, Griswold lit into his friend and only ecclesiastical savior, Rowan Williams, telling him that he "lacked leadership." Then Griswold went on a speaking tour spinning the communiqué to make it mean what he wanted it to mean, with such choice lines as "the communion needs more space to listen" to the plaintive cries of activist gays and lesbians - favorite words of his. Griswold told the leftist *Guardian* newspaper, "I can't imagine a conversation saying we got it wrong. I can see a conversation saying we should have been more aware of the effect that the decisions we took would have in other places." And this: "It does not mean that our point of view has fundamentally changed." He also said that he could not guarantee that his church would honor a moratorium - "how ultimately these questions will be answered remains with the community itself" - and he made it clear that gay blessings would quietly continue.

Over time, it became horribly apparent. Griswold would never settle for any one truth, or one particular interpretation of the truth. Rather, there were many truths, even contradictory "truths" that could and should be held together in tension, without the need to come down absolutely on any one side or the other. To hold things in tension was to live comfortably with ambiguity, even doubt. To say you knew or that Jesus was 'the way, the truth and the life' was to demonstrate an arrogance that he could not support or condone. What might be true for you might not be true for someone else, and one should be prepared to absorb the other truth or simply to live alongside it because one might encounter the mystical 'other' in another person, and to miss that might be sin. Conversely to say Jesus is the only way might be true for us as Christians, but we should never suppose that God had not spoken in other ways, through other persons and we should be "humble" enough to accept that.

Griswold had a way of making one feel guilty even "fundamentalist" to say that we could know the Christian Faith to be true at all times, in all places. For Griswold, this denied the essential character of the "other" that he was and is so fond of.

As pansexuality became the consuming preoccupation of the church, its House of Bishops, clergy and laity, Griswold slowly sank into a sort of cosmic despair, telling one reporter, "I find the endless fixation on sexuality, and more specifically homosexuality, a distraction from other areas that, quite frankly, are matters of life and death. When I retire as presiding bishop, I hope that I'm known for something other than this issue."

Regrettably, that was not to be the case. Homosexuality had become the defining issue and Griswold its *eminence grise,* later emerging from the shadows becoming its most outspoken ecclesiastical advocate, even, at one point, filing an amicus brief on behalf of two gay men caught in *flagrante delicto* in the state of Texas.

What was initially a nominal acceptance of Griswold, became for many, over time, a hardening hatred for the man. Canon David Anderson of the American Anglican Council, expressed it for many when he said that while he recognized Griswold's leadership, "We acknowledge it to have been a fairly disastrous leadership so far, and we are hoping that there might be some changes in the course of direction of the Episcopal Church. We'd love for him to step down and recognize the damage he's done." Consciously or subconsciously, Anderson spoke for tens of thousands of orthodox Episcopalians. The lines had hardened, perhaps forever. In March of 2005, just before she died, Diane Knippers, president of the Institute for Religion and Democracy, called on Griswold to resign. She said he was succumbing to anger "melt-downs".

A 2016 Forum: The Blending of Katharine Jefferts Schori And Frank Griswold

At a forum at the Virginia Theological Seminary in May 12, 2016, the two former Presiding Bishops came together to talk about The Episcopal Church and its future.

Virginia Theological Seminary was celebrating its new chapel, which many saw as an ostentatious circle of creepy New Age architecture. There are no crosses on the walls, the altar had been moved out.

Out walked Bishop Griswold and Jefferts Schori looking like mirror reflections of each other in black pants and careful facial expressions. A small aging crowd was present.

Griswold started off with the rhetorical device of attack by mentioning an article titled, "Bishop as martyr." He then presented himself as a victim, saying that a bishop is the "focal point of people's discontent" and can be seen as the "devil incarnate."

Jefferts Schori said that her spiritual director thought she was "pontifical" in her gifts when she tried to build connections. Pontifical? Who uses that word outside of the pope?

From this apparent lack of humility, we learned that Griswold is a "martyr" and Jefferts Schori is "pontifical."

Jefferts Schori said on multiple occasions that she was about "blessed diversity." She provided no idea what this vacuous phrase meant or was about.

Griswold talked about all the problems that African Anglicans had caused the Anglican Communion. He blamed the Church Missionary

Society and said that the missionaries shared a similar and mistaken theology. "They focused on the bible." That was a huge mistake, according to Griswold.

When asked about the lack of youth at church, Jefferts Schori said that it was good that not many kids went to Sunday School. Her reasoning seemed to be that at Sunday School they might also hear and read the Bible.

A questioner asked Griswold if he believed in heresy, which seemed to imply that Griswold was a heretic.

Griswold gave his definition of heresy, "Are you clinging to a reality because if you don't, you will fall apart? Is it a generous reality?"

Griswold offered nothing about Christ, of course.

The highlight of the evening came, when a man sitting quietly in the front row, said he had a "parochial" question. He cited the primate putting the three years of suspension on the Episcopal Church. He said, "ACNA might be taking our place in the Anglican Communion."

Then the questioner hit on a nerve directly.

He asked; "In retrospect, would you do anything differently?"

Griswold immediately went into a humanist overdrive response about the Anglican Communion. "We are patient, we participate, and we do not cut off relationships."

Jefferts Schori said, "Relationships continue to grow." She stated that there is not "intense conflict." She said that "ultimately relationships will decide" this situation and "that's exciting."

Then the moderator stood up and called everything off. No dialogue allowed. No more questions.

Jefferts Schori and Griswold looked offended by the last question. Perhaps Griswold felt 'martyred' and Jefferts Schori felt her 'pontifical gifts' should not be questioned this way.

The last questioner looked surprised at how they did not interact with his question. He stood up and said, "I think it is grounds for concern." Then he walked quickly out of this New Age venue.

A young man was overheard to tell his friends, "This church has about 30 more years before it is dead."

Jefferts Schori proclaimed "blessed diversity!" again and again without ever defining or even hinting what this phrase meant. She just proclaimed it. Her voice made it sound like the Insiders knew what she meant and to ask more about it would prove that you were an outsider.

She also made a joke about the Second Coming twice. "We won't agree until Jesus comes again!"

What was deafening at the event that advertised itself as the future of the Episcopal Church was the complete lack of any mention of the new Presiding Bishop Michael Curry's 'Jesus Movement'. In fact, Griswold only used Curry's name one time in passing. Jefferts Schori did not mention him at all.

A questioner again asked; "In retrospect, would you do anything differently?"

Merely shrugging this question off, their answer came through as "Nothing."

Griswold's Vision and Future of The Episcopal Church

As the Episcopal Church shrank, questions were raised about its long-term health and future. "Maybe this is the desert time", Griswold opined when asked. For the Episcopal Church and mainline Protestantism, this may be a wilderness period, a time of being shaped, formed and made ready to enter the Promised Land, he said.

The Episcopal Church and the Protestant mainline in America today may be going through a normal "paschal pattern" -- a dying and a rising -- that all churches go through, and that is not necessarily a bad thing, he said.

"There's an arrogance and a self-confidence that is shattered by things falling apart, but beneath the church's many challenges is an invitation to deeper wisdom, a hidden grace that leads to new insight, wisdom and resurrection.

"To use an image from the Old Testament, maybe this is the desert time. The desert was a period of purification and self-knowledge in order that they were prepared to enter the Promised Land. If we are in fact the body of Christ, limbs of Christ's risen body, we're OK," he said.

Griswold's theology had triumphed. Many Episcopalians now travel to that place beyond good and evil, dancing around, shedding biblical morality and belief in the One Lord and Savior of the universe. C. S. Lewis called this "our self-intoxication."

"We are winning!" many Episcopalians now exclaimed in a mad rush of self-centered glory. It was pure foolishness.

As the Church unraveled, Griswold sent a belatedly modified message. "My basic task is to keep as many people at the table as possible, and to remind everyone that though they have their own particular point of view, there are others who have another point of view, and they are equally members of the church, loved by God, members of Christ's risen body, and therefore must be taken with full seriousness. And it's in the tension, often, that the truth, whatever it may be, gets more fully revealed."

In 2005, as his tenure as Presiding Bishop drew to a close and the Episcopal Church was coming apart at the seams with thousands of laity fleeing the church and with orthodox rectors in one diocese after another fleeing their revisionist bishops, Griswold is now being viewed as a leader with shredded theological clothes. Like Richard Nixon, Griswold does not exist outside his role, apart from The Episcopal Church: take his clothes off, he would be invisible. There is one Griswold only, trying desperately to be all things to all people, trying to be what people want. At the same time, he lacked the stamp of place or personality because at some level he is a fictional person, made up of many invisible parts, emerging from the ecclesiastical ether that no theological tradition in church history has ever or would ever recognize. What, after all, is an Affirming Catholic? It's as though he had been sucked out of a cathedral by a giant vacuum cleaner only to discover, when opened, that the vacuum bag was empty. There was no there, there.

KATHARINE JEFFERTS SCHORI

The End of Orthodoxy

"The de- Christianization characteristic of the modern age is, to a large extent, the product of the infidelity of the Christians to their own faith." – Emil Brunner

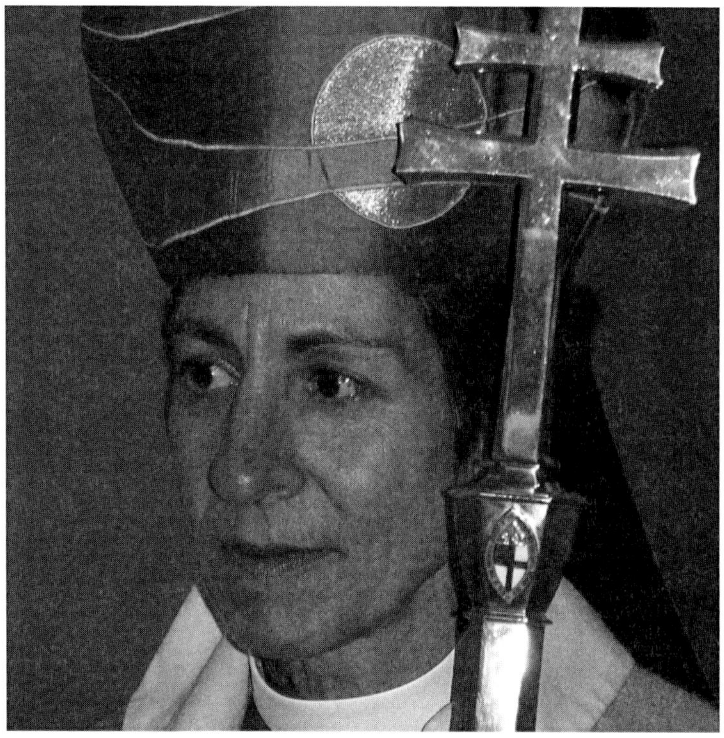

Katharine Jefferts Schori was ordained to the Episcopal priesthood in 1994. She was ordained just 12 years after leaving a career as an oceanographer.

In 2001, she became Bishop of Nevada. On June 18, 2006, she was elected on the fifth ballot at the Columbus, Ohio, General Convention as the first woman to lead a branch of the worldwide Anglican Communion. Jefferts Schori became the 26th Presiding Bishop of the Episcopal Church.

Even though nobody thought Jefferts Schori had a prayer of being elected, many said they'd vote for her on the first ballot just as a way of saying, 'You go, girl! Thank you for being in this mix and for being such a wonderful human being and bishop.'

When results of the first ballot came back, Jefferts Schori was leading with about half the votes she needed. By the second ballot, when all these 'courtesy' votes were expected to melt away, she'd added another five or six votes. With the third ballot, she'd picked up another fifteen votes and then led for the rest of the way.

Many Episcopalians at the Church's Triennial General Convention cheered the largely unexpected choice of Bishop Jefferts Schori, 52, the lone woman and one of the youngest of the seven candidates for the job. Her election was a milestone for the Episcopal Church, which began ordaining women only in 1976. She succeeded Presiding Bishop Frank T. Griswold.

The mood at her installation was hopeful. Most seemed to think they were heading for true enlightened leadership by following her.

Dozens of congregations and priests along with a number of bishops had left the Episcopal Church. Primates overseas threatened schism, with many coming to the rescue providing episcopal cover and oversight to these fleeing parishes and

Dioceses. Bishop Jefferts Schori was a supporter of Bishop Robinson's election in 2003 and the Episcopal Diocese of Nevada permitted the blessing of same-sex unions. Those remaining orthodox dioceses saw her election as a big red flag waved in their faces.

Her election only further strained relationships with three Anglo-Catholic dioceses in the Episcopal Church that refused to ordain women as priests and bishops.

However, she held out an olive branch hoping to mend any breaks and fissures that her election and her positions on issues might cause.

"Alienation is often a function of not knowing another human being," she said at a news conference after her election. "I have good relations with almost all the other bishops, those who agree and those who don't agree with me. I will bend over backwards to build good relations with those who don't agree with me."

"I'm thrilled," said lesbian priest, the Rev. Susan Russell, president of Integrity and an advocacy group for gay and lesbian Episcopalians. "I'm a cradle Episcopalian. I remember when there were no women priests. I remember when they said the church was going to split over the ordination of women. What we're giving as a Father's Day gift to the Anglican Communion is a woman primate, and that is wonderful."

However, some questioned her lack of experience as a church leader, especially of a large diocese, and how it would now be tested by the tensions in her denomination.

"Can she run a big ship of state?" asked the Rev. William L. Sachs, director of research at the Episcopal Church Foundation, the church's analysis arm. "She is certainly smart enough, and she gets it. But can she translate that into an actual program?"

Some critics were quick to focus on her sex, asserting that her election was an affront to others in the denomination who opposed the ordination of women. They described it as further evidence of the church's drift from the shared beliefs of the greater Anglican Communion.

"In many ways the election speaks for itself," Bishop Robert W. Duncan Jr. of Pittsburgh said in a statement. Bishop Duncan was the moderator of the Anglican Communion Network, a theologically conservative group of Episcopal dioceses. "For the Anglican Communion worldwide, this election reveals the continuing insensitivity and disregard of the Episcopal Church for the present dynamics of our global fellowship."

Her election threw in doubt whether three dioceses — Quincy, Ill.; Ft. Worth; and San Joaquin, Calif. — would any longer be permitted to resist the ordination of women. One priest, The Rev. H. W. Herrmann, rector of St. John's Episcopal Church in Quincy said Presiding Bishop Jefferts Schori would not be welcome in his church.

The bigger issue facing Jefferts Schori was the fight over ordaining more openly homosexual priests and bishops. The Pandora's Box of sexualities had been opened, there would be no turning back.

In October 2004, a committee appointed by Rowan Williams, the Archbishop of Canterbury, issued what became the Windsor Report in an effort to head off possible schism in the Communion over the growing sexuality debate. The Report recommended that the Episcopal Church apologize for the consecration of Bishop Robinson, stop blessing same-sex couples and place a moratorium on the election of future homosexual bishops.

On February 12, 2008, the Archbishop of Canterbury announced the formation of the Windsor Continuation Group (WCG). The WCG was formed to address the remaining questions around the Windsor Report and the various formal responses to the Windsor Report from the provinces and instruments of the Anglican Communion. The WCG was chaired by Bishop Clive Handford; Jefferts Schori was on the panel.

The commission responded to the Windsor Report with recommendations that were less stringent. A committee at the General Convention had been struggling to amend those recommendations, which had yet to come to a vote before the clergy and the lay deputies.

It was criticized by liberals for seeming to take for granted that the actions of New Hampshire and New Westminster—and homosexuality in general—were wrong. For example, while it calls for both conservatives and liberals to apologize for disunity, it acknowledges that the conservatives may have acted out of a sense of duty. However, it conceded no such acknowledgement to New Westminster and New Hampshire.

In the end, The Windsor Report never came to a vote in The Episcopal Church.

In 2006, the Archbishop of Canterbury, Rowan Williams, established the Covenant Design Group (CDG) to draft a covenant for the Anglican Communion. The CDG met between 2007 and 2009, producing three successive drafts: the Nassau Draft Covenant (2007), the St. Andrews Draft Covenant (2008), and the Ridley Cambridge Draft Covenant (2009). Each draft was indebted to previous ecumenical covenants that Anglicans had either proposed or adopted.

The final text of the covenant was sent to the provinces of the Anglican Communion in late 2009. As of June 2012, only seven provinces of the Anglican Communion ratified the Covenant, two rejected it, the Church of England and the Episcopal Church of Scotland.

July 11, 2012, the Episcopal Church chose neither to accept nor reject the Anglican Covenant. They opted for a "pastoral response" that recognized the "wide variety of opinions and ecclesiological positions" within the province.

Inquisition

There were any number of situations that Katharine Jefferts Schori should have and could have handled differently that might have made a difference to the outcome, but it was not to be.

Under her leadership the Episcopal Church began to come apart at the seams with priests and bishops fleeing in all directions from what they now believed was a heretical and apostate Church. Jefferts Schori now began to show her true colors.

As they departed, and at her direction, those same bishops and hundreds of priests experienced an Inquisition that they never dreamed would happen. She charged them with "abandoning the communion of the Episcopal Church." (In truth, it was not the Church universal or the faith they were abandoning, but the Episcopal Church and what it had become in moving outside and beyond the historic Christian faith.) She engaged with the courtroom and lawsuits rather than with faith, hope, and love. Jefferts Schori exercised a destructive presence that shocked many and destroyed what was left of an orthodox and biblical, indeed historical understanding of the Christian faith in the Episcopal Church.

Who will ever forget Jefferts Schori's first National Cathedral service with lithe and svelte dancers springing here and there with gorgeous and colorful ribbon banners? But it was her sermon that raised eyebrows and evoked deep concern.

During the formal seating of the new Presiding Bishop, Katharine Jefferts Schori began her sermon telling of the mystical experience of the Frenchman Jacques Fesch. Jacques had killed a policeman during the course of a botched robbery in Paris in 1954. While in prison, he experienced God in a dramatic moment. He wrote about it later saying, "I was in bed, eyes open, really suffering for the first time in my life. . . It was then a cry burst from my breast, an appeal for help—My God— and instantly, like a violent wind which passes over without anyone knowing where it comes from, the spirit of the Lord seized me by the throat. I had an impression, said Jefferts Schori, of infinite power and kindness and, from that moment onward, I believed with an unshakeable conviction that has never left me."

Jefferts Schori's interpretation shocked her listeners. "We might say that saints are those who find a home 'on the way,' in the course of following Jesus. And sometimes the encounter is very much like being seized by the throat. . . Some of us have to be seized by the throat or thrown into the tomb before we can begin to find that depth of compassion."

An odd silence fell over her audience after she proclaimed this story. 'God seizes us by the throat and throws us into a tomb!'

True to her sermon, life within the Episcopal Church started becoming a 'tomb' after rumors spread of her personal Inquisition and destruction of Episcopal churches not perfectly in line with her message. The church had fallen into an abyss of creepy occurrences and the church learned more about her from court documents than it ever learned from the Church's Standing Committees.

Jefferts Schori immediately started attacking conservative Episcopalians that were disaffiliating from TEC. In 2005, she informed Virginia Bishop Peter James Lee that the National Church had a stake in the fight over parishes that were fleeing his jurisdiction and moving to the Convocation of Anglicans in North America (CANA), a missionary body of the Church of Nigeria that had dual jurisdiction with the Anglican Church in North America (ACNA). Jefferts Schori stated that she, as the Presiding Bishop, needed to be personally involved with the property issues as Episcopalians and Anglican separated from each other.

In court testimony she said she would rather sell church properties for "saloons" than sell them to other Anglican jurisdictions and ministries. Over time, properties were sold to start up evangelicals, fundamentalists, even to Muslim Imams for mosques.

She started legal proceedings resulting in churches scattering in all directions trying to get away from her tyranny. Millions of Church dollars were spent under the watchful eye of the Church's legal Doberman, David Booth Beers and his law firm.

She and Virginia Bishop Peter James Lee now fought with tactics that rose to a new vicious cutting edge. There would be no mercy shown to those who left. The properties would be fought in every legal venue open to the church; salaries and pensions would be cut off and priests inhibited and deposed.

In 2006, the large charismatic Virginia churches started leaving the Episcopal Church.

On January 22, 2007, the Diocese of Virginia headquarters sent out a sad letter saying that Peter Lee's previous strategy of dialogue, entreaties and deal-making would now end. Lee stated he would inhibit the ministry of twenty-one priests because they had abandoned the Communion of the Episcopal Church. The list included names that many held in high regard.

Katharine Jefferts Schori officially responded to the statement about their departure saying this: "While the Episcopal Church laments the recent votes by some persons in Virginia congregations to leave this church, we are clear that individuals may depart, but congregations do not." This mantra would be repeated again and again over the next difficult year.

The list included among others, The Rev. John W. Yates II, rector of Falls Church in Falls Church, VA, a powerhouse evangelical congregation that ministered to Washington's political and northern Virginia's business elite.

The axe also fell on The Rev. John A. M. Guernsey, who would later become a bishop in the Anglican Church in North America.

A new and sad day had opened for the Episcopal Church with the beginning of multiple court cases. On January 31, 2007, the Diocese of Virginia filed lawsuits against eleven congregations. Jefferts Schori's reign of terror had begun.

She solidified her personal power by her many successful lawsuits. She inspired fear and loathing in those who crossed her path.

On April 25, 2007, Jefferts Schori said in an interview to the Boston Globe that the Episcopal Church has a vocation to keep "questions of human sexuality in conversation, and not just before our own church, but for the rest of the world."

She went on to say that society in Africa was fifty years behind the United States in development. "Where the protestors are in some parts of Africa or in other parts of the Anglican Communion today, is where this church and this society we live was fifty years ago."

Between 2003 and 2007, the Episcopal News Service reported that some 165 parishes had left the Episcopal Church. Hundreds more would follow. Moreover, in 2007, 43 percent of congregations had experienced membership declines of 10 percent or more over the past five years. Jefferts Schori had disciplined or deposed ten bishops of the Episcopal Church. Of their own volition, four bishops had left the Episcopal Church for the Roman Catholic Church. Eighty-three priests had been inhibited or deposed. The Episcopal Church was engaged in about fifty-six lawsuits against churches, priests, vestries or dioceses when they attempted to leave the Episcopal Church.

Pittsburgh Bishop Robert Duncan

Jefferts Schori then accused the highly regarded Bishop of Pittsburgh Robert William Duncan of abandoning the communion of the Episcopal Church.

This would turn out to be the worst ecclesiastical blunder in her tenure and a watershed moment. She had unleashed a lion who would not be tamed or intimidated by her. Ordained a priest in 1973, Duncan was consecrated bishop of the Diocese of Pittsburgh where he served from 1997 until his ouster in 2008.

Almost immediately, Jefferts Schori began proceedings against the evangelical catholic bishop, deposing and stripping him of his consecration. Her preemptive actions surprised many. However, time would reveal that she had a tiger by the tail and the tiger would not be scared off.

Duncan set in motion something that had never been successfully achieved before – an alliance of evangelical and Anglo-Catholic dioceses that would cement and grow a new Anglican denomination on North American soil. In time, he would become the first primate and archbishop of the Anglican Church in North America (ACNA), beginning June 2009 until his retirement in June 2014.

In September 2008, Presiding Bishop Jefferts Schori successfully inhibited Duncan's ministry. based on the accusation that he had abandoned the church. A divided Episcopal House of Bishops voted to remove Duncan by a vote of 88 to 35, with four abstentions. She had already pronounced him guilty, then had a trial to again pronounce him guilty.

Episcopalians could now watch depositions on YouTube from their formerly dignified church premises.

At one point, a lawyer asked a tense Jefferts Schori, "Do you believe that there is estrangement in the Episcopal Church?" Jefferts Schori replied that the "level of acrimony has increased" between the Episcopal Church and ACNA. She asserted, "ACNA is a further provocation to the Episcopal Church."

The lawyer continued, "Do you view ACNA as a threat to the Episcopal Church?" She replied, "It is a challenge."

Bishop Mark Lawrence and the Diocese of South Carolina

When Jefferts Schori looked at the situation in the Diocese of South Carolina, she saw a personal affront not only to her authority but to what she believed about truth itself.

Many believed the diocese was leaving TEC over the ordination of an openly homosexual bishop. That was not entirely correct. The diocese separated in 2015, nine years after TEC elected its first, non-celibate, gay bishop - and only after the denomination tried to strip all authority from its bishop, the Rt. Rev. Mark Lawrence.

The real issues, opined Canon Jim Lewis, were rooted in the 1970s, well before Gene Robinson became the first openly homosexual Episcopal bishop in 2003. "It's About God, Not Gays," he cried.

"To understand the situation in South Carolina, you need to understand the history of the Episcopal Church, which is the American expression of the Anglican Communion.

"We have a unique view of the denomination since the Diocese of South Carolina was one of the nine pre-existing dioceses that founded TEC in 1789. The denomination has been redefining itself since the 1970s effectively evolving into two churches under one roof - a traditional one that embraced historic Anglican doctrines and a modernist one.

"By the 1990s, the modernist faction was gaining dominance within the denomination. For example, TEC's then-Presiding Bishop, the Most Rev. Frank Griswold, proclaimed that "truth," is "pluriform."

"This meant the church recognized no single truth, no single theology, no single pathway to salvation. He effectively said that one person's truth is as good as another's. And many of us found that to contradict everything we believe as Anglicans.

"It's true that we live in a nuanced, multicultural world, but traditional Anglicans believe in the authority of Scripture. For us, a belief in Christ is fundamental to the faith, not one of several optional paths to salvation. It is why we are Anglicans, rather than Unitarians or Buddhists or Hindus or something else."

In a 2006 interview with TIME magazine, Jefferts Schori, a strong pluriform proponent, claimed that to believe, as Jesus said, that He is "the way the truth and the life no one comes to the Father but through Him," was to put God in an "awfully small box."

For those departing TEC, that denial of Jesus' essential role clearly displayed the difference between traditional and modernist or pluriform Anglicans/Episcopalians.

The denomination's embrace of relativism only increased under Jefferts Schori's leadership.

As the newly elected Presiding Bishop, Jefferts Schori presided over the General Convention in 2006 that failed to honor the requests made by the Anglican Communion and the Windsor Report.

In response, seven dioceses - including the dioceses of South Carolina, San Joaquin, Calif.; Pittsburgh, Fort Worth, Quincy, Ill., Dallas and Central Florida - asked the Archbishop of Canterbury to grant them oversight by someone other than TEC's presiding bishop.

When no action took place, an exodus began. San Joaquin left TEC in 2007. The Diocese of Quincy, Ill., voted to leave in 2008. Pittsburgh and Fort Worth left in 2009. Three dioceses remained, including Dallas, Central Florida and South Carolina.

Between 2000 and 2010, TEC church attendance dropped by 23 percent - and some dioceses lost up to 80 percent of their attendees at Sunday services. Beyond the four dioceses, more than 100 individual parishes left the denomination. The Diocese of South Carolina stayed, trying to work with TEC. "We took the steps necessary in good conscience to differentiate ourselves from the positions and actions of the TEC leadership while still remaining in the denomination," said Lewis.

"It's true that our people were torn about TEC's shift away from historic Anglican beliefs, but we remained part of the denomination, until last year, when it ruled that Bishop Lawrence had "abandoned" the church and took steps to remove him from the leadership role to which members of the diocese had elected him."

The denomination's Disciplinary Board for Bishops claimed that Bishop Lawrence had abandoned the Episcopal Church "by an open renunciation of the discipline of the church." The decision stemmed from the bishop's consistent efforts to protect traditional voices and beliefs. The charges laid against him were for actions taken by their Diocesan Convention and its duly elected leaders.

The Diocese of Mark Lawrence's Standing Committee announced that the action of TEC's Disciplinary Board triggered two pre-existing corporate resolutions that simultaneously disaffiliated them from the Episcopal Church. They called a special convention of the diocese.

In November 2012, the disaffiliation was affirmed by the vast majority of members who attended the special convention. It was confirmed again in votes by congregations within the diocese. In all, 49 parishes representing 80 percent of the diocese's 30,000 members voted to leave TEC, exercising their right to freedom of association.

Anglican leaders from around the world sent messages of support for the diocese. Many members of the global Anglican Communion felt as they did that TEC had departed from historic Anglican beliefs. Most agreed TEC had embraced a radical fringe scriptural interpretation that made following Christ's teachings optional for salvation.

The Diocese of South Carolina had also been visited by numerous Anglican bishops to demonstrate their support. More than a dozen bishops from around the globe have been their guests since their departure. The truth is there were vastly more Anglicans in Communion with the Diocese of South Carolina than there were with the Episcopal Church.

In January 2013, the diocese filed a suit in South Carolina Circuit Court, asking for legal protection of the diocese's property and identity from takeover by TEC. Critics suggest that their suit was unusual. Some even said that the litigation was unprecedented - and "un-Christian." However, the only thing unusual about the lawsuit was that the breakaway diocese managed to file its lawsuit before TEC.

At this point in time, TEC had filed more than 80 lawsuits seeking to seize the property of individual parishes and dioceses that left the denomination.

The Episcopal Church admitted to spending more than $22 million on its legal action. These efforts were largely successful when TEC attempted to seize the property of individual parishes. Parishes across the country were then evicted from their churches.

TEC's policy remained simple and punitive: No one who left TEC may buy the seized church buildings. In several cases where TEC succeeded in seizing a church, it simply evicted the congregation and shuttered the building. In some cases, the church was handed over to remnant groups that remained loyal to TEC. In other cases, the church was sold to another religious group.

Over time, TEC began to have less and less success with the lawsuits it filed against a number of dioceses. An Illinois Circuit Court judge decided that TEC had no grounds to seize the endowment funds of the Diocese of Quincy.

On July 24, 2014, the Diocese of Quincy won a major victory against The Episcopal Church and the Episcopal Diocese of Chicago after nearly six years of litigation. There was a two-week trial complete with more than 15,000 pages of exhibits, including the Nicene Creed.

Could a diocese retain ownership of its assets after seceding from a denomination? In reflecting on this litigation, retired Bishop Keith Ackerman referred to Quincy, which was the smallest of the Episcopal dioceses, as 'the mouse that roared.' The answer was yes.

With more than 50 wins under its belt, TEC suffered a decisive defeat with the ruling coming out of the Adams County courthouse. The trial court held that there is no provision in TEC's Constitution or Canons which require prior approval by the Episcopal Church of a diocesan constitution or its canons. There is no express prohibition against withdrawal of a diocese.

In a unanimous opinion, the Appellate Court also rejected TEC's claims and held that TEC failed to prove that it was hierarchical. It further ruled that the hierarchy was not necessary, since the property dispute could be decided using neutral principals of law.

In Texas, the Supreme Court overturned a lower court decision supporting TEC over the separated Diocese of Fort Worth. In South Carolina, a federal district court judge decided that the Circuit Court of South Carolina was the proper court to decide the fate of the property, upsetting TEC's efforts to get the case heard by the federal judiciary.

It's About Religious Freedom

Leaders in the Diocese of South Carolina felt they had no other recourse for their protection. They believed that, much like St. Paul's appeal to Rome (Acts 25), they felt confident the courts would give them a fair hearing. While TEC attempted to portray them as bigots, the real issue was religious freedom.

Members of the diocese who voted to leave TEC believed the denomination had moved away from the authority of Scripture and their historic Anglican beliefs. "They left us. You may agree with us about this, or you may find that TEC's revisions are appropriate. But whatever you believe, those personal opinions should not prevent us - or others - from practicing our faith," said their leaders.

And, since religious freedom is constitutionally guaranteed in the United States, they believed that the people who built and paid for the disassociated parishes and dioceses had a right to their property.

Obviously, TEC wanted to keep those millions of dollars in property - an attractive prize for a denomination that was losing members and closing churches.

The Irony of Bede Parry

In 2004, the then Bishop of Nevada, Katharine Jefferts Schori, received a former Roman Catholic priest, Bede Parry, as a priest into the Episcopal Church. What made this issue explode in Jefferts Schori's face and into the Episcopal Church is that Parry had sexually abused minors under his care as a Catholic priest. As a result, he had been barred from exercising his ministry in the Roman Catholic Church, and this was known to the Bishop of Nevada when she received Parry into TEC.

How was it possible that a former Roman Catholic priest who had admitted to repeated abuse of minors under his care and who agreed to be laicized, could have been received into TEC as a priest was startling. Furthermore, the Diocese of Nevada acknowledged that it was aware of his past misconduct, including a police report, prior to his reception, but offered up reassurances that the bishop and Commission on Ministry had decided that he did not pose a risk to children.

A later psychological evaluation made by the Roman Catholic Church shortly before Parry began his process of reception into TEC, found that Parry had a "proclivity to re-offend with minors!" Once his past conduct became public knowledge, Parry immediately tendered his resignation as a priest in TEC. This resignation was characterized by the Episcopal News Service as Parry's "renouncing his orders"!

TEC and the Diocese of Nevada's bishop Dan Edwards tried to spin it that the diocese and national church had "followed the applicable canons…" but that was too disingenuous by half.

Canon lawyer Allan Haley concluded otherwise and wrote that there were indeed canonical violations in this process.

That the Diocese of Nevada and the Office of Public Affairs could knowingly receive into TEC's priesthood a child abuser while complying "meticulously" with all canons, policies and procedures was hard enough to take. At the same time the Presiding Bishop was pushing out the front door orthodox priests and bishops, but allowing a known child sex abuser to be priested, coming in by the backdoor was mind blowing.

At one point, Bethlehem Bishop Paul Marshall weighed in and said Jefferts Schori threatened bishops not to reveal multiple sexual abuse cover-ups.

Commenting on the Bede Parry affair, Marshall said, "Now let's be serious. When 815-level lawyers threaten and cajole diocesan bishops not to reveal multiple sex-abuse cover-ups at the highest level lest former leaders be embarrassed, what can we expect, and why do we look down on the Roman Catholic Church?

"As a rector I had to follow a priest who was simply passed along by another bishop, and as a bishop have had the same experience with a staff member who was protected by his bishop, with catastrophic results here.

"On paper, we are a one-strike church, but in reality, too many people have walked. 815 (national church headquarters) refused comment on this story with principled-sounding obfuscation. There is no more transparency at 815 than previously, as some commentators know to their pain."

In an e-mail to Virtueonline, Marshall wrote, "The anger has subsided for the moment, and I come to the office incredibly sad. As you know, I think we are doomed as a church unless our life is vigorously centered in the Gospel and see our mission in only those terms that are consistent with it." The bishop said he and his staff were planning on writing a full-length piece (and eventually a book) on this subject. To date, the book has never been written.

Bede Parry died on Nov. 27, 2013.

Bishop Heather Cook

Fast forward to 2010 and the tragic story of the Rev. Heather Cook, yet another example of political, or should we say female correctness, as Jefferts Schori was determined to fill the Church hierarchy with women at every available opportunity.

In 2010, on the Eastern Shore of Maryland, a sheriff's deputy saw a car careening down a road. The drunken driver drove partially in the road, partially on the shoulder of the road, and the car had badly shredded tires.

The trooper stopped the car. The driver was a woman. On the seat next to her, he noticed a bottle of wine, a fifth of whiskey, two baggies and a metal instrument used to smoke drugs. The car reeked of alcohol and burning rubber. Vomit dripped down her shirt and polluted the air in the car.

The deputy administered a blood alcohol test and got a blood alcohol level of .27. He arrested the woman and in the process of booking her discovered she was a Maryland Episcopal priest.

As court documents are public records, Episcopal leaders read the court records. What did they do with this information? They should have cooked the Rev. Cook's goose. They should have stopped her ministry altogether and taken immediate disciplinary action against her and made this information public. They didn't. Cook was a dangerous woman and should not have been working with people or remotely near a pulpit.

Instead, Cook got away with it. Even more horrifying, they set about promoting her to become a bishop.

In May of 2014, Heather Cook was elected as the next Suffragan bishop of the Diocese of Maryland. The website trumpeted the news. "Cook is the first woman to be elected a bishop in the Diocese of Maryland." A FIRST! That's important.

This suggested to every American priest with ambitions to the episcopacy; Buy a bong and get your bishop nomination. Cynical. Not necessarily.

Leaders controlling the election process knew about Cook's reckless and dangerous drinking and drug use and said nothing, covering it up entirely. No mention was made of it to the laity voting for her.

Before Cook's consecration, Maryland Bishop Eugene Sutton informed Katharine Jefferts Schori that Cook was drunk at a private dinner. Jefferts Schori did nothing, continuing her reckless path of public consecration of a besotted, wannabee bishop. No one spoke out. No one didanything about it. It is the silence of the lambs.

The Presiding Bishop then proceeded to consecrate Heather Cook a bishop, even knowing full well that Cook had fallen off the wagon.

In front of a congregation of trusting Episcopalians, Jefferts Schori affirmed that Bishop Cook was to be trusted and followed. Cook arose from her fancy consecration with titles, honor and money. She was suddenly an instant celebrity in American ecclesiastical and episcopal culture.

Then, on the afternoon of Dec. 27, Heather E. Cook, now the second-highest ranking bishop in the Episcopal Diocese of Maryland, got into her Subaru Forester and began driving and texting through the affluent Baltimore neighborhood of Roland Park. Police later measured her blood alcohol level at 0.22, nearly three times the legal limit.

It all came apart. She slammed into a bicyclist, the father of two small children, and, as he lay dying, gunned her car and fled the scene of the accident. She fled, leaving Thomas Palermo to die alone and his two children fatherless. Cook consumed this man's life without a thought for him that tragic day. She thought only of herself, perhaps a reflection of Jefferts Schori's own leadership style.

Another cyclist saw Cook's Subaru's crashed front end, realized she was probably the driver, and tried to talk to her. Cook bolted without letting him finish. That cyclist chased her to the gated community where she lived. Thirty minutes later, after pleading from her own bishop, she returned to the accident scene.

On Feb 4, 2015, Bishop Heather Cook was indicted on 13 charges including automotive manslaughter and driving under the influence. Cook, 62, was convicted on four criminal charges in killing the cyclist and served just over half of the seven-year sentence she was given.

So, what did the Episcopal Church do? Katharine Jefferts Schori said she could not say anything because there was a confidential disciplinary action going on. Cook got still more confidentiality. She got confidentiality about the 2010 arrest, then she got confidentiality after she killed a cyclist. The question must be asked, when do churches have rights to information?

Following this, Maryland Bishop Eugene Sutton issued a shocking statement. He declared that the church would continue to serve alcohol. Sutton said we would not want to be compared to "Puritanism."

The Rev. Gay Clark Jennings, President of the House of Deputies, said that the Episcopal Church needed "to repent for our role" because of the "systemic denial" about problems with alcohol and drugs. This, as it turned out was only one of many problems and denials in the Episcopal Church.

It took the *Baltimore Sun* newspaper joining the chorus of outraged voices to personally protest Jefferts Schori. They published fact after fact about Jefferts Schori's tenure as Presiding Bishop, pointing out that she had endangered all Baltimore citizens by her unethical consecration of the besotted Heather Cook.

Jefferts Schori's Violent Theology

Katharine Jefferts Schori exposed her non-Christian theology in her book *The Heartbeat of God* (Skylight Paths Publishing, 2011). Her interpretation of Bible stories is disturbing. All of her biblical interpretations are based on a life of promiscuity and violence. She says that these are the same lives of people in the Bible who show us the Way to Christ.

One example is where she refers to Jesus as a "Hell Angel's gang leader" (p.115) and a "party animal." (p. 4)

For those not familiar with American culture, Hell's Angels are a violent and drug-using motorcycle gang. A party animal is used for someone who is frequently drunk or using drugs.

Her "theology" was never challenged by the House of Bishops; she skated through unscathed. A more serious group would have had her tried for heresy.

Her other attacks on people in the Bible include the following.

From the book of Ruth, Naomi is the pimp sending Ruth over to have sexual relations with Boaz. Jefferts Schori writes that Naomi told Ruth "to hightail it over there and 'uncover his feet'—Another euphemism—and to lie down beside him." She continues saying that, "Today's equivalents of Ruth and Naomi [are] your women who are being trafficked or groomed for exploitation." (33)

Jefferts Schori taunts the destruction of Sodom and Gomorrah saying that Lot's wife is turned into salt "who hesitates as they flee from Sodom, which God aims to destroy for its abysmal lack of hospitality. (Genesis 19:20-26)" (60). Jefferts Schori refuses to admit that the problems are the sexual sins of men that God will ultimately destroy.

Jefferts Schori refers to the leper who wanted healing as "whiny" (22). That leper is a man suffering from one of the worst diseases ever and she makes fun of him.

Indeed, she uses inappropriate sexual image of seduction to describe the relationship of God with humanity. She writes that people are "*lured* into relationship with love." (117)

She outdoes herself when she writes, "God works through 'inappropriate sexual behavior.'" (31) Christians know that God does not approve, work through or bless inappropriate sexual acts such as incest, rape, and molestation. Her violent imagery avoids any sense of right and wrong.

Her predecessor Frank Griswold had scrapped the notion of absolute right and wrong, thus opening the way for this nonsense. Now, according to Jefferts Schori, God works through inappropriate sexual behavior.

Perhaps in her deluded mind, God works through their (WHO IS "THEIR"?) sexual behavior because this is some sort of revelation to them, or a game-changer meant to apply to all of us so that we don't feel guilty about anything. Jefferts Schori seems to condone inappropriate sexual acts, because God is going to work through it anyway. Or, to paraphrase song writer Stephen Stills, 'love the one you're with,' even if they don't want it.

All three Presiding Bishops, Browning, Griswold and Jefferts Schori believe God works through anything because God is not personal and nice. This is not hyperbole to them. God is applying taser shocks to your souls.

In the strange odyssey of Jefferts Schori's theology, God does the following;

Grabs us by the throat

Drinks until drunk

Stuns us with electrical shocks

Let's all sorts of odd sex go on and works through it.

Throws us into a tomb

Offers a pacemaker jolt (xiv and 91)

But Jefferts Schori tells us that God is like this, or so her book informs us.

In her own way, Jefferts Schori surely did much to add to human suffering. She seized numerous church buildings away from worshipping Anglican communities. She threw many decent, godly priests under the bus because deep down she hated what they believed. She described Jesus as a violent gang member and party animal.

She writes, "God offers a pacemaker jolt to tweak our heart's rhythm." (xiv and 91) She repeats this image multiple times.

Instead of the Christian faith, Jefferts Schori believes that God works like an impersonal machine, jolting and stunning people. This "stun gun" god would destroy all human freedom and leave terror in its wake. Jefferts Schori's images of a violent god jerking, shaking and jolting people are images that need to be rejected as non-Christian.

Only a violent god would want what she offers: intense troubles for fellow Christians. Grab churches away from these Anglicans and they will feel like she has applied electrical prods against their tender souls, their praise-filled love for Jesus.

Even if we ignore her bizarre book, we are still left with the reality that this 'pontificate' does not react normally to protecting people who don't agree with her.

She devalued the Bible. She believed neither in its plenary inspiration nor its authority. She did not see faithful people who willingly kept writing checks while they worshipped in a Church that systematically attacked their faith and moral values, one by one.

As she destroyed lives, her internal image of God became more violent, perhaps justifying her own violence against orthodox believers. Her bizarre logic seems to be the following: God loves her and as she destroyed godly priests, God loved the violent destruction of these conservative people.

Jefferts Schori's Failed Female Leadership

Jefferts Schori became the high 'pontifical' priestess of human destruction in the Episcopal Church.

She gave her stamp of approval to the consecration of a tragic and drunken bishop like Heather Cook, who killed the father of two in a drunken moment in time. Then Jefferts Schori tried to turn Episcopalians into people of her book and worshipping her blessed diversity. Jefferts Schori was the natural successor to Griswold, the man who had successfully paved the way and carried her on a Sufi wave beyond right and wrong.

Bishop Jefferts Schori defrocked, humiliated and destroyed hundreds of Anglican priests. It was the bonfire of the Episcopal vanities.

Two examples were the late Bishop of Washington Jane Dixon's legacy. In a long fight with a tiny Accokeek Parish in Southern Maryland, Dixon picked a fight with a small-town rector who did not recognize female bishops. The diocese spent over a million dollars in legal fees pursuing this one priest. Dixon could not start or grow churches, so she consumed them.

The later Washington Bishop Mariann Budde at her consecration and first service had the New Age and atheist poet David Whyte read out loud; his ramblings were heard in her sermons. It had slipped her mind that she had been ordained to preach the Word of God from holy writ. These women were the products of Katharine Jefferts Schori.

The culture honors firsts and TEC wanted to be in the forefront with women and their newfound rights. TEC wanted to have the first female bishop, first female dean of a seminary, first bishop to take small parishes to American courts, first female to ignore the scriptures and use odd poetry in the Washington National Cathedral. Over time it would only get worse.

Jefferts Schori's Blessed Diversity

Jefferts Schori pushed the Episcopal Church down the same road Frank Griswold had wanted it to go, that of unity with other religious traditions.

She writes, "The Abrahamic religious traditions uphold a vision for the healing that is, of human beings individually as well as in community, their relationships to the divine, and the relationships among all the various parts of creation. That vision is variously called *tikkun olam*, the repair of the world, shalom, salvation, or the reign of God. Shalom in Hebrew, or salaam in Arabic, is a kind of shorthand for that prophetic dream of a healed world, and it underlies the ancient prophetic insistence on the need for multiple forms of healing, leading to a world of justice and peace. In modern Jewish circles, *tikkun olam* has become synonymous with the notion of social action and the pursuit of social justice."

What is striking here is the equality she lists between the Islamic, Jewish and Christian theological terms. There is nothing distinctive about the role of Jesus Christ as mediator, Savior or Lord of history or Lord of the universe. In fact, there seems to be no need of a mediator. This was a totally non-Christian understanding of our relationship with God the creator. But this is where pluriformity ultimately led.

Jefferts Schori went even farther than this, in an interview in TIME magazine, July 10, 2006, when she talked about Jesus. "We who practice the Christian tradition understand him as our vehicle to the divine. But for us to assume that God could not act in other ways is, I think, to put God in an awfully small box."

In an NPR interview, Robin Young asked Jefferts Schori, "…Scripture says that Jesus is the Light and The Way and the only way to God the Father." [National Public Radio, Here & Now Interview, New York, Nov. 2, 2006]

KJS: "Christians understand that Jesus is the route to God…that is not to say that Muslims, or Sikhs, or Jains, come to God in a radically different way. They come to God through…human experience… through human experiences of the divine. Christians talk about that in terms of Jesus."

RY: "So, you are saying there are other ways to God?"

KJS: "Human communities have always searched for relationship that which is beyond them…with the ultimate…with the divine. For Christians, we say that our route to God is through Jesus. Uhh . . . uh . . .that doesn't mean that a Hindu . . . uh . . .doesn't experience God except through Jesus. It says that Hindus and people of other faith traditions approach God through their own cultural contexts; they relate to God, they experience God in human relationships, as well as ones that transcend human relationships; and Christians would say those are our experiences of Jesus; of God through the experience of Jesus."

RY: "It sounds like you're saying it's a parallel reality, but in another culture and language."

KJS: I think that's accurate . . .I think that's accurate."

In her own words, Jefferts Schori states that many different paths exist to God and Jesus is only one of them. Jefferts Schori is trying to fragment and destroy the Christian vision and make the Episcopal Church part of a polytheistic schema. Her Inquisition left the Episcopal Church a decimated and desolate place. People fled from her church over her aggressive and violent leadership.

Jefferts Schori's Heresies

During her tenure, Jefferts Schori uttered numerous heresies that in other denominations would have gotten her thrown out of the Church.

She rejected many of the Articles of Religion including Article XVIII. "Of obtaining eternal Salvation only by the Name of Christ. For Holy Scripture doth set out unto us only the Name of Jesus Christ, whereby men must be saved."

She also rejected the The Lambeth Quadrilateral, The Lambeth Conference of 1888. Resolution11. (a) The Holy Scriptures of the Old and New Testaments, as "containing all things necessary to salvation," and as being the rule and ultimate standard of faith.

On the Consecration of a Bishop, she could not for a moment have believed this, "Are you persuaded that the Holy Scriptures contain all Doctrine required as necessary for eternal salvation through faith in Jesus Christ? And are you determined out of the same Holy Scriptures to instruct the people committed to your charge; and to teach or maintain nothing, as necessary to eternal salvation, but that which you shall be persuaded may be concluded and proved by the same?"

She also rejected the specific words of Jesus who said, "I am the way and the truth and the life. No one comes to the Father except through me." John 14:6 (NIV)

"... If you confess with your lips that Jesus is Lord and believe in your heart that God raised him from the dead, you will be saved." Romans 10:9

Comments and interviews by the Presiding Bishop of The Episcopal Church revealed a common theme: she no longer (if she ever did) believe in the unique claims of Jesus Christ as both Savior and Lord, resulting in a poor, if non-existent Christology.

In a video interview, Jefferts Schori openly and publicly denied that Jesus is the only way to salvation. http://www.youtube.com/watch?v=_IxG96wpx60

She has publicly said that Muslims do not need converting to Christ and that she would never tell them they do, and that Jews are saved under the first covenant. In her most recent statement, uttered publicly at General Convention in Anaheim, she stated that personal or individual conversion (to Christ) is a Western heresy and likened it to "work" rather than that of free grace.

In a video, she clarified her views on salvation saying, "In some parts of Christianity we have turned salvation into a work, you have to say that I claim Jesus as my Lord and Savior in order to be saved and that turns it into a work and it denies the possibility of grace."

The former Suffragan Bishop of Albany, The Rt. Rev. David Bena, blasted Jefferts Schori at an ACNA Council in Herndon, VA, where he is now a full bishop in communion with the Anglican province of Nigeria. Bena said that Jefferts Schori's rejection of personal salvation is a heresy that insults our Heavenly Father, who wishes each one of us to have a personal, saving relationship with his Son.

"Perhaps this leader has not read, marked, heeded and inwardly digested Romans 10:9, 'because if you confess with your lips that Jesus is Lord and believe in your heart that God raised him from the dead, you will be saved' and a thousand other passages from the scriptures covering the same subject are there," he cried.

During her occupation as the titular head of the Episcopal Church for nine years, she uttered more heresies recorded by any sitting bishop, with the possible exception of John Shelby Spong and more by Charles E. Bennison, Bishop of Pennsylvania, whose line that "Jesus was a sinner who forgave himself" might earn them both a place in the sixth circle (heresy) of Dante's nine circles of suffering located within the Earth.

Over the course of nine years, she variously denied the bodily resurrection of Jesus and the full deity of Christ, referred to Jesus as "mother Jesus" at one point and said St. Paul should have listened to a demoniac girl for spiritual guidance.

She was the perfect ecclesiastical piñata. Hit her hard enough and out would pour more heresies.

"The crisis of this moment has several parts…the overarching connection in all of these crises has to do with the great Western heresy – that we can be saved as individuals, that any of us alone can be in right relationship with God. It's caricatured in some quarters by insisting that salvation depends on reciting a specific verbal formula about Jesus. That individualist focus is a form of idolatry, for it puts me and my words in the place that only God can occupy, at the center of existence, as the ground of all being. That heresy is one reason for the theme of this Convention," she opined.

Then there was this statement of hers; "We Christians often think the only important part of the Jerusalem story is Calvary, and, yes, suffering and killing in that place still seem to be the loudest news. But Calvary was a waypoint in the larger arc of God's dream – it's on the way to Jerusalem, it is not in Jerusalem. Jesus' passion was and is for God's dream of a reconciled creation. We're meant to be partners in building that reality, throughout all of creation." Any notion of substitutionary atonement is washed away in this single statement. No cross, no salvation, we are part of "reconciled creation" that has no basis in the cross. While the whole creation presently groans waiting for redemption, she has it reconciled.

On May 12, 2013, the Presiding Bishop preached in Curaçao, in the Diocese of Venezuela. Jefferts Schori told listeners that the Apostle Paul betrayed his understanding of the faith he had been given and was guilty of bigotry in handling a case of demonic possession found in a slave girl.

The account in Acts 16 reads thus: "Now it happened, as we went to prayer, that a certain slave girl possessed with a spirit of divination met us, who brought her masters much profit by fortune-telling. This girl followed Paul and us, and cried out, saying, 'These men are the servants of the Most High God, who proclaim to us the way of salvation.' And this she did for many days.

"But Paul, greatly annoyed, turned and said to the spirit, 'I command you in the name of Jesus Christ to come out of her.' And he came out that very hour. But when her masters saw that their hope of profit was gone, they seized Paul and Silas and dragged them into the marketplace to the authorities." Acts 16:16-19 (KJV)

Jefferts Schori interprets the story of Paul and the slave girl by accusing the apostle of spiritual blindness and bigotry. She off handedly includes the issue of same sex relationships that the great apostle doesn't even hint at.

Jefferts Schori opined, "We live with the continuing tension between holier impulses that encourage us to see the image of God in all human beings and the reality that some of us choose not to see that glimpse of the divine, and instead use other people as means to an end. We're seeing something similar right now in the changing attitudes and laws about same-sex relationships, as many people come to recognize that different is not the same thing as wrong. For many people, it can be difficult to see God at work in the world around us, particularly if God is doing something unexpected.

"There are some remarkable examples of that kind of blindness in the readings we heard this morning, and slavery is wrapped up in a lot of it. Paul is annoyed at the slave girl who keeps pursuing him, telling the world that he and his companions are slaves of God. She is quite right. She's telling the same truth Paul and others claim for themselves.

"But Paul is annoyed, perhaps for being put in his place, and he responds by depriving her of her gift of spiritual awareness. Paul can't abide something he won't see as beautiful or holy, so he tries to destroy it. It gets him thrown in prison. That's pretty much where he's put himself by his own refusal to recognize that she, too, shares in God's nature, just as much as he does - maybe more so. The amazing thing is that during that long night in jail he remembers that he might find God there - so he and his cellmates spend the night praying and singing hymns."

One blogger said that sermon in Venezuela is probably "the worst sermon ever".

Five Marks of Mission

Jefferts Schori proclaimed the Five Marks of Mission as her theology and goal.

To proclaim the Good News of the Kingdom. TEC had totally failed to proclaim the Good News about Jesus. Jefferts Schori saw the "Good News" as climate change. It was not about redemption through the blood of Christ at the cross.

To teach, baptize and nurture new believers. What new believers? TEC was and is hemorrhaging parishioners at a fast clip, with no sign of a let up. Jefferts Schori saw no irony in this.

To respond to human need by loving service. Minimally true. TEC doesn't come close to agencies like World Vision, Food for the Poor, Food for the Hungry, the Salvation Army et al. in "loving service."

To seek to transform unjust structures of society, to challenge violence of every kind and to pursue peace and reconciliation. This begged the question of what unjust society TEC has transformed. Jefferts Schori had steadily taken a lop-sided view of the Arab-Israeli conflict by promoting the Palestinian side, only refusing to sell stock in companies that do business with Israel. After all, she didn't want to tick off the Republicans in TEC who pay the bills and who actually support the State of Israel.

A reporter described the false theology of the Presiding Bishop in a sermon Jefferts Schori delivered at the United Thank Offering Ingathering, Festival Eucharist at General Convention in 2012.

"On July 8, 2012, Presiding Bishop Katharine Jefferts Schori preached her brand of post-Christian religion while masquerading as a Christian bishop. She mocked most of the crucial doctrines of the Christian faith, including the God of creation, the Incarnation, and the Trinity. She accomplished this through her demeaning use of rhetoric. She taunted the Lord by the use of the name "Big Man" and then pointed her finger at everyone listening and told them that they have "missed the boat." She then proclaimed that she has the answer for this. We all need the "act of crossing boundaries" to become God after which our hands become a "sacrament of mission."

"As seen in her sermon Jefferts Schori decided that she is beyond the discipline of rational thought. She makes up fictional information about Jesus when she states definitively about his unknown earlier years, "He [Jesus] has never stood up in their synagogue before and said anything particularly challenging."

"Jefferts Schori continues her fictional theology that Jesus wants us 'to tend the garden we share with all the rest of creation.' She also demeans the Roman Catholic Church in her reference to the toy 'Nunzilla' that is a contemptuous stereotype of nuns as aggressive and mean. In a spirit of criticism, Jefferts Schori also lumps together without differentiation all members of the Senate and House of Representatives, saying that people speak of the "contempt and arrogance they hear from Congress and other politicians." Jefferts Schori's contempt for others seemed to know no bounds.

"Jefferts Schori asserted that humans are to boldly cross the frontier to become God and by doing so denies the truth of the once-for-all Incarnation. Instead, we all become God and 'start building the world that God intended at creation.' Jefferts Schori presents the reality of God as so weak that the 'Big Man' intended something and could not carry it out and so we becoming God are going to succeed where God did not.

"It is now apparent that Jefferts Schori draws inspiration from Darwin's destruction of boundaries between the human being and animals. Charles Darwin erased the boundary between humanity and nature in his Descent of Man in 1872 by blending these two distinct groups together. For those who follow Darwin's thought, humans lost their position of being created in the image of God with an eternal soul. As the boundary between humanity and animals was erased, humanity becomes only one more species of animal.

"Jefferts Schori leaves a wide wake of destruction behind with this sermon: the eternal triune God has been torn down, human beings are to boldly claim our place as God, and the sacraments of the Eucharist and Baptism have been turned into things our hands make. In other words, Jefferts Schori accepts that now humanity, animals and God are one undifferentiated blob. This is essentially a form of solipsism, the belief that self is all that is known to exist. Anyone can see that this is both pure heresy and utter nonsense."

The Presiding Bishop totally emasculates the text, making it mean what she wants it to mean; not what it implies or even says.

The retired Bishop of South Carolina, The Rt. Rev. Dr. C. FitzSimons Allison, expostulated that Mrs. Jefferts Schori's remarks are not a distortion of Christology, the Trinity or even the Creed, but are the announcement of a different religion. "It doesn't measure up to heresy. She is trying to reduce Christianity to the blank space in the creed between the Virgin Mary and Pontius Pilate."

The Four Humiliations of Katharine Jefferts Schori

On June 13, 2010, Jefferts Schori got publicly smacked down in England, as the Episcopal Church's chief ecclesiastical officer when she was told she could not wear her miter in Southwark Cathedral.

She called the requirements "nonsense" and said "it is bizarre; it is beyond bizarre."

The Church of England did not allow women bishops at the time, so it would have violated their canons to recognize her as a bishop and to function as such. So, she spoke only as a priest.

The invitation by Dean Colin Slee to the cathedral was a calculated snub to Rowan Williams. Permission for Jefferts Schori's visit was sought by Slee, subject to the standard rules applying to any minister ordained overseas to which the US Presiding Bishop is no exception.

It also appeared to be timed to coincide with preparations for the Church of England's own debate on women bishops in York.

Added to this first humiliation is that the objections voiced by clergy in the Diocese of Southwark to Jefferts Schori's visit were based on her heretical views of Christian doctrine and Holy Scripture.

Jefferts Schori was further humiliated when she was told she had to provide evidence of her ordination to each order of ministry, a requirement based on a 1967 Act of Parliament.

But the hypocrisy of the situation is that two visiting Anglican Archbishops from Nigeria and Uganda and one bishop from Bolivia to the U.S. were denied the right to preach and celebrate Holy Communion at Church of the Good Samaritan in Paoli, PA.! Why should she get better treatment in London?

She did the next best thing. She carried her miter in hand down the cathedral nave -- no doubt to make the point that she had been publicly humiliated and she would push the issue right to the edge of ecclesiastical correctness. The incident became known as Mrs. Jefferts Schori's Mitregate.

The second humiliation she experienced was a public rebuke she got from the liberal Primate of the Anglican Church of Southern Africa, Thabo Makgoba. It came when she spoke at the USPG Missions Conference in Swanwick, England.

Makgoba, who is also the Archbishop of Cape Town, accused her of not listening to views about homosexuality from the Global South. He also offered up the view that sexuality should be seen as a "second place" issue and that his province was an example of how Anglicans stayed together amid their differences about human sexuality. "Listening" was the great mantra of Presiding Bishop Frank Griswold.

Jefferts Schori had no option but to take the slap; any rebuff would have been met with charges of racism.

A third humiliation occurred at the Swanwick (USPG) conference when she was asked by one leading woman cleric present, an archdeacon, why she was acting so divisively. The question, delivered at a private meeting, brought forth applause from many of those present.

The fourth humiliation came when she was asked to step down from her seat on the Standing Committee of the Anglican Consultative Council, and also (apparently) to absent herself from the next Primates' Meeting the next January in London.

According to Canon lawyer Allan S. Haley, the Archbishop of Canterbury made a private request to the Presiding Bishop to step down. Jefferts Schori refused him.

The press officer to the Secretary General of the Anglican Consultative Council later confirmed to The Church of England Newspaper that Canon Kenneth Kearon had hand delivered a letter from Dr. Williams to Bishop Jefferts Schori at the April 17 consecration ceremony of Bishop Ian Douglas of Connecticut.

The gulf between the Presiding Bishop and the Archbishop of Canterbury had widened, irretrievably.

Williams had called for the removal from certain inter Anglican ecumenical commissions of representatives from those provinces in the Anglican Communion who had formally broken one of the three moratoria called for by the Windsor Report and the last Lambeth Conference since they no longer represented the mind of the Communion. This was a clear rebuff and humiliation to the Presiding Bishop.

"Hell hath no fury like a woman scorned," and Mrs. Jefferts Schori has had that in spades.

It was the religious leaders of his day who Jesus accused of blasphemy. Might not the same condemnation apply to the likes of Jefferts Schori for her blatant denial of the unique claims of Christ?

She concluded her ad hoc remarks by saying, "It is not my job, and it is God's job to figure out who is going to be in the Kingdom." While it is true that we do not know WHO will be in the kingdom, there is no doubt about HOW one obtains entrance into the kingdom. The Presiding Bishop is not free to pronounce on the sovereign "work" of grace which God does in the lives of people who often privately repent, seeking his forgiveness away from the bright lights of public crusades, weepy public confessions and much more. God works in the heart, far from human observation.

Katharine Jefferts Schori's blunt universalism does not sit well with Scripture nor with historic Anglicanism. No serious Christian theologian, excluding Arius, in twenty centuries has challenged the unique claims of Jesus being fully divine, that he is fully God and fully man, the Savior of the world, Messiah (that one's for the Jews), prophet, priest and king who will one day spread his rule over all the kingdoms of the earth, and of His kingdom, there will be no end.

Jefferts Schori espoused that in some parts of Christianity, we have turned salvation into a work that denies the possibility of grace. One wonders what 60 million evangelical Anglicans in the Global South would make of that statement? It is why GAFCON was ultimately formed to counter the growing heresies in the West, especially from its presiding bishops.

Jefferts Schori is right on one point. She said comments like these "drive some Christians nuts." In this, she is absolutely correct. It drove Evangelicals and Anglo Catholics right out the Church doors to safer spiritual climes. Orthodox Anglicans in the Global South reeled from her statements.

If the HOB had any theology at all, it would have brought her up on heresy charges. That did not happen, because most bishops, who had gone through the church's liberal Episcopal seminaries in the last 30 years, don't believe much more differently.

After all, if Walter Righter could take a walk over heresy charges that he ordained an avowed non-celibate homosexual man to the priesthood, and if no one is going to bring presentment charges against Bishop John Shelby Spong whose 12 theses denied every vestige of historic Christianity, why bother going after Jefferts Schori? If the HOB were to do so, there would be cries of feminist outrage ranging from charges of sexism and exclusivity to fundamentalism.

Jesus' words in Matthew 12:30-32, might certainly apply to Mrs. Jefferts Schori; "Whoever is not with me is against me, and whoever does not gather with me scatters." The Episcopal Church is being scattered to the four winds by moral relativity, blatant theological apostasy and much more.

Among her numerous heresies was to exchange the call of The Great Commission (to preach the gospel to all the world) for Millennium Development Goals, what she said personal salvation as a "Western heresy" and a "work", why millions of dollars were spent on litigation expenses that in no way advanced the Kingdom, and why the apostasies of TEC went unchecked, resulting in millions leaving the church.

Her farewell speech week was a picture of subterfuge, lies and spin.

"I am deeply grateful for what God has been up to in the midst of our journey together."

That "journey" cost the Episcopal Church a loss of nearly 200,000 Average Sunday Attendance) ASA members and tens of millions of dollars in lawsuits for properties that the courts are now granting to those departing TEC. Her ultra-liberal, theologically-challenged credentials earned her the dubious title as the Church's first dictatorial female Presiding Bishop of the Episcopal Church. She managed to alienate the entire Anglo-Catholic wing of the Church and most of its evangelicals.

She left a church in rapid decline with more than two-thirds of the church made up of women over 60. A third of TEC's rectors are women. None of the women priests and bishops have shown any ability to make the Church grow, preferring to sound off on the platitudes of social reform rather than the gospel of Jesus Christ.

Katharine Jefferts Schori was the continuation of the Gadarene slide of The Episcopal Church. There would be no turning back.

On "that Day" it may well be too late for "personal salvation" for Katharine Jefferts Schori.

PRESIDING BISHOP MICHAEL CURRY

On June 27, 2015, at St. Mark's Episcopal Cathedral in Salt Lake City, Utah, at the 78th General Convention of the Episcopal Church, the House of Bishops elected North Carolina Bishop Michael Curry, 62, in a landslide vote to be its new and first Black Presiding Bishop.

Curry garnered 121 votes out of 174 voting bishops to become the Church's 27th Presiding Bishop. He won on the first ballot. An hour later, the House of Deputies voted overwhelmingly by 800 to 12 affirming that election. Curry was considered a moderate bishop following in the ultra-liberal footsteps of Katharine Jefferts Schori.

Curry stepped into the position at a time when the Episcopal Church claimed little more than two million baptized members and an average Sunday attendance of 657,102.

Bishop Curry's election came at a time when the denomination had lost 200,000 active members since 2003, when an openly homosexual priest living in a partnered relationship was consecrated a bishop in the Episcopal Church, in the Diocese of New Hampshire. The Episcopal Church had faced open rebellion from its orthodox wing, with thousands of Episcopalians fleeing in numerous denominational directions.

The president of The Union of Black Episcopalians, (UBE) Annette Buchanan approved the election, saying, "We are overwhelmed, excited... we never thought in our lifetime that we'd live to see a black president of the United States and a black presiding bishop. Presiding Bishop-elect Michael Curry is a longtime UBE member."

At a press conference following his election, the new black Presiding Bishop dodged bullets on his new role. No significant change of direction was envisaged for the Episcopal Church despite much new talk of "evangelism" and "discipleship".

A reporter asked the newly elected Presiding Bishop directly if he was an evangelical, to which Curry replied, "I am a follower of Jesus."

For those of orthodox persuasion listening, it was a tip of the hat, perhaps an inkling of what the Church might expect, even as his preaching revealed the old-style cadence of black preachers. He would not be solidly orthodox in faith and morals. He would be a different shade of gray. His education, however, was solidly white, with a BA from Hobart and William Smith College, and an MDiv from the Berkeley Divinity School at Yale. He had also studied at the College of Preachers, Princeton Theological Seminary, Wake Forest University, the Ecumenical Institute at St. Mary's Seminary, and the Institute of Christian Jewish Studies. Michael Curry had lived for the most part in a white man's world.

His performance as bishop of North Carolina had not been stellar. He took office in 2000. In 2003, the year figures were first recorded there were 48,957 baptized members. It rose by 2.1% to 50,009 in 2013. Average Sunday Attendance (ASA) -- the true health of a diocese, saw a significant decline from 16,765 in 2003 to 14,729 in 2013 a drop of 12.1%.

The state itself had grown to a point that it is nearly 10 million today (9.94 million in 2014) up from 8.63 million in 2005. His diocese had not reflected the growth of the state.

The Bishop and Homosexuality

Bishop Curry had already declared his hand on pansexuality.

The spiritual leader of nearly 50,000 Episcopalians in North Carolina had, in 2004, given his formal blessing to churches in his diocese to bless same-sex unions. In a letter to clergy, Bishop Curry said, "the blessing of the committed life-long unions of persons of the same gender is one way our community can live the Gospel through faithful and loving pastoral care and spiritual support for each other." No priest, he said, is obligated to perform same sex weddings.

In 2004, the Diocese of North Carolina suffered a severe budget crisis. It faced a shortfall of over $1 million caused largely, critics say, because of the policies Curry had chosen to pursue and the way he had chosen to implement them. It was the year after Bishop V. Gene Robinson, an openly homosexual, was elected Bishop of New Hampshire. Curry openly and publicly embraced that ecclesiastical action.

In November 26, 2003, 12 orthodox priests in his diocese wrote Curry, laying out their concerns, distress and sadness for his support of the ordination of Robinson and his vote to acknowledge the blessing of same sex unions as a part of the common life of the church. They expressed their gravest concern.

> We believe you are in serious error, and that your leadership of this diocese and the broader church is sorely hindered by your acceptance of beliefs contrary to the Word of God, and by teaching these beliefs to your flock.

The 12 twelve priests said that the teaching of Scripture and the Universal Church was clear -- that the union of a man and a woman in marriage is the will of God for sexual expression.

They blasted his interpretation of the Old Testament moral codes and said his move to exempt the moral law of the Old Testament along with the ceremonial and temporal laws was wrong.

> The creation account, the Holiness Code, and the Lord Jesus speak with one voice. Our Anglican forebears acted wisely in giving us Article VII. Analysis of the pertinent texts shows conclusively that the Old Testament moral laws are valid for Christian believers.

They ripped the bishop, concluding their letter saying;

> To say that Jesus loves everybody, including homosexuals---is true! Homosexual orientation is never condemned in scripture. It is the practice of non-marital sex that Jesus proscribes. Here is where we come to one of your major mistakes. We are not free to make Jesus into someone who would bless whatever relationships we chose ---just so long as we feel love. Jesus teaches us over and over that our loves are disordered. He showed us that we must not trust ourselves. Fallen humans need to be taught a new life where we love what God loves and hate what God hates.

In public statements, Curry had said that the New Testament texts regarding homosexual expression should be dismissed because those texts are about abusive relationships.

The 12 priests rebutted this saying,

> You should have known better. Plato (in the 5th century BC), Philo and Josephus (both writing in the first century AD) and

> many others wrote clear and detailed records describing loving, lifelong same sex relationships. The Mediterranean world of late antiquity was a pagan world where same sex relationships were celebrated and common. This is why Paul, the cosmopolitan, well-traveled Jew, takes on the issue of homosexual practice - most famously in the first chapter of his letter to the Romans. The horizontal example of human depravity is homosexual activity, a practice so unnatural and so unhealthy as to be obvious.
>
> We are most concerned for the homosexual community, believing you have given them warrant to practice a form of sexual expression that the scripture describes as sin.

Curry's view on homosexuality is also at odds with the vast majority of black pastors in America and with the vast majority of Anglicans in the Anglican Communion whose archbishops had fought long and hard at several primatial gatherings against Frank Griswold's push for homosexual acceptance.

But opposition to Curry's position had also come from some 34,000 black American clergy who said, after the Presbyterian Church USA endorsed gay marriage, "Don't equate your sin with our skin."

Homosexuality for Curry would now no longer be the white man's burden. It would be his to bear with pride as he leads a church whose establishment credentials he will wear with equal pride and a gay button of approval on his lapel. In truth, Curry had now inherited the whirlwind and he would find himself caught in the ebbs and flows of history and a church that is disintegrating beneath his feet.

Curry and The Episcopal Church

On first appearances, Curry seemed humble and genuine, exuding an air of deprecating humor as he talked meaningfully of the need for more evangelism and discipleship. Those are conservative buzzwords, but they can mean something quite different to the ears of Episcopalians who eschew traditional understandings of evangelism as "exclusionary", "fundamentalist", "happy-clappy" or even homophobic. There is no talk of conversion, it is all about inclusion. The sinners' prayer is not to be found on the lips of parishioners, clergy or bishops in the Episcopal Church.

Evangelism means being open to absolutely everybody...gays, straights and now, because the numbers are slipping, even allowing unbaptized persons' access to Holy Communion, a violation of canon law (1.17.7). But these are desperate times for clergy and bishops as parishes and dioceses wither and shrink. There is a wink-wink, nod-nod to what is euphemistically called "open table." Come as you are, stay as you are, was the accepted wisdom.

Curry believed in the Church being inclusive of all, especially African-Americans and Africans of the diaspora. "Inclusive" is also the language of gay and liberal agit-prop. However, inclusion has not made Episcopal churches grow. Conversion had been ruled out, making the Church's future bleak.

Echoing an old spiritual, Curry said during a video that "our hand must be on the Gospel plow." Noble words, but what do they mean in an Episcopal context? 98% of Episcopal bishops do not believe in traditional understandings of the word "gospel". Good News means to include not convert, because to truly convert means to "separate out" from those who do not believe. There is no such animal in the mind of an Episcopal priest or bishop.

"We are followers of Jesus -- Jesus of Nazareth -- and the truth is we've got a message to proclaim, a life to live and something to share and offer the world," said Curry. "There's a lot of suffering in this world. There's a lot of heartache, there's a lot of nightmare. We are people who believe that God has a dream and a vision for this world, and that Jesus has shown us how to follow him in the direction of that and how to help this world live into God's dream and vision for us now," said Curry.

It was here that Curry introduced the term the Jesus Movement. "Our work is actually the work of participating in the Jesus movement, which seeks to realize God's dream and seeks to accomplish God's mission in this world."

Many reporters thought this meant the "Jesus Movement" founded on the West Coast of the United States in the late 1960s and early 1970s that spread primarily throughout North America, Europe and Central America, before subsiding by the late 1980s. Members of the movement were called Jesus people, or Jesus freaks.

This, as it transpired, was not what he meant. The interpretation of his words is the world of New Testament scholarship, which had adopted the term "Jesus Movement" to describe the first generation of followers of Jesus in Palestine. The term even took Jefferts Schori by surprise at the press conference as the name of Jesus was rarely found or heard on her lips. Realizing "God's dream" and "accomplishing God's mission in this world" is the ether or Star Trek language of Jefferts Schori and could be taken to mean almost anything from opening coffee houses in Atlanta to building herb gardens in Honduras.

"The church must help form disciples who will live like Jesus," said Curry.

Curry gave a hint at what he calls evangelism. "After formation, there's evangelism and I know sometimes folks are afraid of that word, but I'm not talking about evangelism like other folk do it," he said. "I am talking about the kind of evangelism that is as much listening as it is sharing." Being present with another person and listening to that person is a "transforming possibility" of invitation and welcome.

When asked what strategies he would employ to address the 24% loss of membership in The Episcopal Church in the last decade, he said, "None! Questions about church attendance and church decline are second-order questions."

But where does the proclamation of the Good News about Jesus and the call for repentance and faith come in? Curry did not say.

When asked by one reporter how he would he go about healing the divisions within the Episcopal Church between evangelicals, traditionalists and liberals, Curry delivered the standard mantra -- made famous by Frank Griswold, that he would be the Presiding Bishop of all

Episcopalians. His door would be open to everyone. It was pure fiction, of course, but everyone bought into it, at least for a time.

VOL posed two questions to the Presiding Bishop-elect. The first was would he move to end the property litigation that has cost the national church some $60 million dollars and more to date. He quickly looked over his shoulder at Jefferts Schori and then said he would continue her policies. When asked how he planned to heal the rift (broken communion) between TEC and the Global South, Curry countered by saying that he had several Anglican friends in the Global South, but he would not say if they included any archbishops or bishops. "I am committed to the work of reconciliation...an agent of God's reconciliation in any way I can. I will do my best."

Curry was, in part, able to distance himself theologically from Jefferts Schori. Schori could not affirm the bodily resurrection of Jesus, said personal faith was a Western heresy, and avoided using the name of Jesus in an Easter or Christmas message -- multiple times.

For Curry, the bar was higher in distancing himself from her.

Curry and His Crazy Christians...transforming the world

Curry talked about his Jesus Movement brand throughout the Episcopal Church.

On April 3, 2016, he spoke at the President's Church, St. John's Lafayette Square, directly across from the White House. St. John's has a long tradition of intellectual and thoughtful sermons, akin to policy statements issued by government officials. Many looked forward to this talk as Curry's released statement to put substantial thought into the bare-bone phrase Jesus Movement that was being widely used.

A large crowd assembled at St. John's, waiting for ideas about where the Episcopal Church would be heading under the direction of Presiding Bishop Curry. At the hour-long talk before the worship service, Curry offered the idea that the Jesus Movement will "transform the world." He used this phrase on multiple occasions and in a surprising statement said that poverty could be ended by 2030. He offered no factual support for his belief in this goal. He also briefly addressed the changes in sexual mores. Human sexuality now has become a "game changer," he said.

"We are applying the same teachings of Jesus in some new ways."

The well-heeled and educated congregation listened and at the time for questions, many rose to ask questions about the conflicts within the Anglican Communion. One man asked about the relationships within the Anglican Communion. Then Curry said little, saying briefly that "some relationships have been frayed." He continued, "Most relationships are intact and are thriving."

He added, "The majority of the dioceses and provinces in Africa have not broken relationship with TEC." He then adds, "Three in fact have."

One intent person questioned Curry about whether he was willing to reconcile with ACNA. The interrogator pressed, "How are you going to lead this?"

Curry paused and said that reconciliation with ACNA would take "time and generations." His words implied that reconciliation would take decades.

Curry then told a story about Foley Beach whom he had met recently at the Primates' meeting. He said, "Everyone was watching when we met. We treated each other like human beings." Curry continued with a reference to his recent surgery, "Foley Beach said to me, 'I have been praying for you.'" Curry laughed and reported that he said to Beach, "Were you praying for a swift recovery or not?" Laughing, Curry concluded about this conversation, "We didn't sing Kumbaya."

More intent questions followed, including, "How are you going to keep building this church since we see that no one under the age of 25 is here?"

Curry struggled and offered few ideas about this challenge.

Following the meeting, Curry preached a lively sermon in the historic pulpit. He made his argument for the Jesus Movement, saying, "This world can be a tough place." He became impassioned. "We are people of faith who follow Jesus of Nazareth." He encouraged, "Dare to believe and live to change this world." His summed up his idea about the Jesus Movement saying in a terse phrase, "Just believe!"

Curry also advocated that Christians stop worshipping Jesus, saying, "It is easy to worship him. Get him out of your hair." He also asserted, "It is easy to adore Jesus, but it is contrary to self-interest to follow Jesus."

To support this theology, Curry referred to the Baptist minister Harry Emerson Fosdick, one of the most prominent liberal ministers of the early 20th Century, who said there are two ways of getting rid of Jesus: we can crucify him and we can worship him. Curry gave the impression that Fosdick meant we are not to worship Jesus from our hearts. Yet Fosdick in his writings does not say that but instead asserts the danger of thinking of worship as building churches. This misrepresentation of Fosdick's theology was not cleared up in the sermon or after.

Curry concluded his sermon by telling a long story. "A man was going to walk across the Niagara Falls on a tightrope."

"He stops and asks the crowd, "Do you believe I can walk across this tightrope?"

"We believe!" the crowd yells.

The acrobat took a pole and walked across the tightrope over the falls.

The acrobat then said, "Do you believe I can walk across the falls pushing a wheelbarrow?"

"We believe!" the crowd yells.

The tightrope walker is successful.

"Now do you believe I can walk across the falls pushing a wheelbarrow with a blindfold on?"

"We believe!" they yell.

Again, the man does this.

"Now do you believe I can walk across the falls pushing a wheelbarrow with a blindfold on with someone in the wheelbarrow?"

"We believe!" they yell.

"Do we have a volunteer?"

No one answers. Curry laughed and the congregation joined in.

Then, with passion, Curry said, "Look in that wheelbarrow! Desmond Tutu and Mary Magdalene are in that wheelbarrow!

Curry then concluded this story, saying, "We don't need to have all the answers! Just believe!"

Following this story, Bishop Curry began singing, "He's got the Whole World in His Hands!"

An elegant reception followed in the historic St. John's, Lafayette Square Hall. The policy of the Episcopal Church had been presented. People chatted about Curry's energetic preaching and singing style as well as the idea that parishioners should just believe and accept the game-changing new sexual rules. A few quietly mentioned that addressing tensions in the Anglican Communion was not a high priority for Curry. Poverty could be abolished within 14 years and reconciliation with ACNA could take 50 years. Because of the unlikely reconciliation between the Episcopal Church and ACNA, now questions were raised about what the Archbishop of Canterbury Justin Welby would do about ACNA and its Archbishop Foley Beach. The Jesus Movement seemed to offer new sexual standards, simple belief and plans for massive social change.

Curry is on record as referring to Jesus as crazy. He writes in his book *Crazy Christians*, "Jesus was, and is, crazy! And those who would follow him, those who would be his disciples, those who would live as and be the People of the Way, are called to be exactly that—crazy." Curry also includes Mary Magdalen as crazy.

As the Presiding Bishop of the Episcopal Church, Curry's use of the word "crazy" for the Lord Jesus appears as a rhetorical device to weaken the rational discussion of theological beliefs. In his book he also uses numerous pop culture imagery. He writes about the song, "Put your hand in the hand of the man who stilled the water," but then feels like it helps his arguments if he lists celebrities who have sung this: "Joan Baez, Shirley Caesar, Ray Conniff, the Five Blind Boys of Alabama, Tennessee Ernie Ford, Ramsey Lewis, the Platters, Loretta Lynn." In his installation sermon at the Washington National Cathedral, Curry uses pop culture creations in his use of Kermit the Frog and says, "It ain't easy being green." He also quotes the 1980s popular song, "Don't worry! Be happy!" It seems apparent that Curry is building on the foundation of popular culture and not theological reflection to attempt to reinvigorate the Episcopal Church.

In fact, when Curry describes a spiritual experience of his own, he uses the image of a Salvador Dali painting. Curry writes, "I saw Jesus being transfigured and reshaped, not into something he wasn't, but into a disclosure of who he was and is. In my imagination his shape was altered, stretched, like an image in a Surrealist Salvador Dali painting."

However, we analyze Curry's writings, we get a glimpse of his deep connection to popular and celebrity culture in the United States. His use of relaxed terminology and referring to Jesus as "crazy" and "stretched out" do call his orthodoxy into question.

If TEC is the "Episcopal branch" of the Jesus Movement, (and when was that decided?), one wonders what its priests and bishops have been selling for the last 40 years. The Church has embraced sodomy, homosexual marriage, rites for same and a panoply of sexualities. It has focused on any number of social issues including racism and its approval of abortion. Despite this, there has been no visible uptick in membership or people clamoring to pass through its "The Episcopal Church Welcomes You" red doors. The Episcopal Church is visibly dying, with aging men and women and no replacements coming up through the ranks from millennials or Gen Xers. This is the real-world Curry now faced.

Evangelism, Anti-Racism and White Privilege

Curry, early on, linked evangelism with anti-racism and white privilege.

At the 2012 General Convention, he set out what he called a bold agenda for Episcopalians to work for racial reconciliation and evangelism.

Curry told church leaders to begin the work of racial reconciliation by deeply listening to each other rather than immediately asking staff members to develop new programs. The church's new and continuing evangelism work would now include plans to gather and support the church's hidden evangelists, whoever they were and to revive revivals.

The triennial budget included $3 million for starting new congregations, with an emphasis on Hispanic communities, $2.8 million for evangelism work and funds for a major new $2 million initiative on racial justice and reconciliation.

Hidden behind the fine words was the whole notion of white privilege. Whites should be made aware, if not found guilty, that they must work for racial justice and reconciliation.

The 2012 General Convention attempted to shift the church's focus on racial issues by way of Resolution C019, which gave the Presiding Bishop and the President of the House of Deputies an extraordinary mandate to "lead, direct, and be present to assure and account for the Church's work of racial justice and reconciliation," especially targeting systemic racial injustice.

Resolution C019 acknowledged that racism continues to plague society and the church despite repeated efforts at anti-racism training and other racial justice and reconciliation initiatives, including more than 30 General Convention resolutions dating back to 1952. It called on the church to begin anew.

The outline of a plan to implement C019 "emerged out of listening to each other's stories and hearing the pain and the hope of our culture through our own stories," he said.

Curry believed that it is in that deep level that changes will happen. Taking time to listen to the stories of each other's experiences both inside the church and in the world, he told the two council committees, "in the long run may bear fruit both for our church and our country and for the various countries in which the Episcopal Church is located."

At no time was the church told *who* the racists were in the Church. Presumably every white person was an actual, if not potential racist and needed to "listen" to the stories of those oppressed by Whites.

People were asked to identify other ways to share their stories, develop "reconciling relationships," listen to the church's neighbors (including around the Anglican Communion and in other denominations), and increase formation opportunities for all ages. But who exactly was supposed to be reconciled to whom? The Episcopal Church is 90 percent white and only 4 percent black!

One Episcopal leader astutely observed, "The simple fact is we don't know the racial makeup – or for that matter, really, the gender makeup or age makeup – of the Episcopal Church, and so to speak of reconciliation, to speak of transformation, to speak of righting historical wrongs is hard when you don't know who's here."

Indeed, the call went out to consider a census to gain a clearer understanding of the church's demographic makeup and its historic and current participation in systems of racial injustice.

VOL commissioned a study of women in the Church and found, not surprisingly, that two thirds of the church were women over 60, the other third largely old men and some families. Virtually no Millennials make up TEC's demography. Are all these women racists? The truth is they were more likely to be members of an altar guild than the KKK!

So, it begged the question what and who are the racists and who indeed should be reconciled to whom? The Presiding Bishop offered no answers.

One suggestion was to convene a churchwide gathering to discuss racial justice and reconciliation, similar to the 2011 gathering to discuss same-gender blessings, or perhaps a series of smaller gatherings around the church. The church was told that these meetings would not be about people presenting ways to spend the $2 million. Instead, they would center on "listening for where God is moving, where the wisdom is, what were the best practices and, frankly, how does transformation happen, as we hear deeply how do we become reconciled."

No one knew, not even Presiding Bishop Michael Curry. It sounded like a lot of words thrown together to make people feel guilty for something they had never thought or done, but which a vibrant black presiding bishop was now pushing them to feel.

One Executive Council member said the plan for having the "whole church listen and then speak" is important because of the stories that will emerge. "All of those stories are essential; all of those stories must be heard."

And that will take time.

Gay Jennings, President of the House of Deputies said this was something "for the long haul. It's clear that this is not predominantly or only a black-white issue; [it's clear] that we have a multicultural, multiethnic, multinational church and so that the issues around racial justice and racial reconciliation are extremely complex."

As church leaders made clear at Executive Council, the work of racial justice and reconciliation and the evangelism work to which Convention also called the church are intertwined.

Evangelism

'How about we make evangelism the new normal?'

The Presiding Bishop and others in the church would like to banish to the history books the days when Episcopal evangelism was an oxymoron.

Curry said he can "remember very clearly the days when evangelism was on the back burner and not taken seriously."

Now the Episcopal Church is poised "to take a step to reclaim our heritage as Christians and followers of Jesus in the Anglican and Episcopal tradition" to find and nurture new disciples," he told another group of Executive Council committee members.

"How about we make evangelism the new normal?" a woman leader suggested. Just as there were always Episcopalians doing outreach and mission work with or without committees behind them, there are evangelists already at work in the church. "They're out there, they're hiding; we can welcome them home," she said.

One of the first ways to do that, was an evangelism summit, planned for in Dallas, co-hosted by Forward Movement, to be followed by a conference for the wider church.

"The idea is to build a network of evangelism professionals and others across our church who will be able to carry the Jesus Movement into their local communities," the Rev. Susan Snook, chair of council's Joint Standing Committee on Local Ministry and Mission, explained during the council meeting.

There were also plans to adapt and share existing evangelism formation materials across the church and create new materials where needed.

"Revivals are part of our history," said The Rev. Canon Stephanie Spellers, Canon to the Presiding Bishop for Evangelism and Reconciliation. "We're going to reclaim that part of our history."

While those gatherings would have a dynamic preacher, they would also be about training local teams "to practice relational evangelism and deep listening with their neighbors, schoolmates, friends, co-workers."

"There'll still be an altar call, but this time to church fellowship and neighborhood action," she said in her sermon.

Because the revival ought not be just a one-time mountain-top experience, Spellers said follow-ups will link newcomers to churches and ministries, strengthen those ministries and look for places where new communities of faith might be planted.

Evangelism doesn't just take place face-to-face these days and Convention funded a major digital evangelism initiative. The Task Force on Leveraging Social Media for Evangelism will facilitate the creation of new materials designed to train "digital storytellers for Jesus,"

The church's Office of Communications was tasked to manage a renewed online evangelism effort that would not be about pushing new content but, instead it would try to meet people who come there with their "big questions about God, faith, about community". The effort would use tools such as Google AdWords, Spellers explained. This effort would take place both in English and Spanish.

Convention also envisioned a "churchwide network for planting congregations, training and recruiting planters"; Resolution D005 allocated $3 million for the work, including just more than $1 million for Latino/Hispanic ministries.

Work was underway to update the grant application process for church plants and more Mission Enterprise Zones.

The work also involved ways to increase accountability and assessment and be more proactive in recruitment of people and places, Spellers said. And the budget included a new missioner for new church planting capacity to join with the Rev. Thomas Brackett, the Episcopal Church's missioner for new church starts and mission initiatives.

Snook described the new position as "another laborer in the vineyard" and Spellers said, "without more infrastructure, without growing staff capacity, we are just throwing the seed of grant money on dry, shallow soil."

Those involved also wanted to develop a "community of practice" among church planters and other evangelists because "it can be very lonely work," Snook told the council.

The members of council heard over and over again that, in all the interconnected work of evangelism and racial reconciliation, collaboration across the church and with like-minded people in other churches is essential.

"This is not a moment for competition," Spellers said. "The days of competition between denominations are over. It's a moment for collaboration for the sake of the Jesus Movement."

In an interview with the Charlotte Observer, in October 2015, Michael Curry offered up his agenda on how he planned to run the Episcopal Church after Jefferts Schori.

He offered up his definition of evangelism. It is: [He plans] to promote a form of evangelism that calls on members to listen to others' faith stories and then share their own.

Such evangelism, Curry said, isn't about converting people -- "that's God's job, not ours" -- but is about helping them "find their way to God."

He also wants to stress the love of Jesus, foster social justice, work for reconciliation -- racial and otherwise -- and preside over a church that's open to all, including both supporters and opponents of same-sex marriage.

Sharing stories is fine, but that is not evangelism. No one will dispute hearing how people come to faith in Christ, if that indeed is what the Presiding Bishop-elect means, is a good thing. Testimonies of faith, "once I was blind, but now I see" and similar stories are indeed welcome.

But Curry has stated he has a different understanding of evangelism.

Winning people for Christ is at the heart of the gospel. Evangelism might be a dirty word to some people. In some quarters, it is clearly an embarrassing word especially for liberals and revisionists who prefer words like "inclusivity," "diversity," and "interfaithery."

The truth is evangelism is the good word about Jesus. It is about proclaiming the Good News about Jesus, his life, death and resurrection straight at the heart of its cultured despisers. It is telling people, graciously, that they are lost without Jesus. It is saying the hard word that we are all sinners, not merely by our acts, but we are born in sin - it is in our genes and DNA. Only through Christ's shed blood can we be released from the penalty of sin and made right with a loving God.

That's the only kind of evangelism the Bible proclaims. Unless Bishop Curry is prepared to state that unapologetically, his understanding of evangelism falls short and the Episcopal Church will go on selling a gospel that is no gospel at all. It will continue to wither and within two generations be out of business.

Stressing the love of Jesus is fine, but without mentioning the atoning death of Jesus being at the heart of God's love, then "love" becomes a squishy word and ultimately meaningless. "God loves absolutely everybody," Louie Crew often opined. But loving everybody won't save everybody.

We are children of God by birth. We are sons and daughters of God by reason of the New Birth.

Curry's understanding on fostering social justice, while noble, is not the centerpiece of the church. Article XII: Of good works (one of the 39 Articles) says this:

"Albeit that good works, which are the fruits of faith and follow after justification, cannot put away our sins and endure the severity of God's judgement, yet are they pleasing and acceptable to God in Christ, and do spring out necessarily of a true and lively faith, insomuch that by them a lively faith may be as evidently known as a tree discerned by the fruit."

So good works are not what puts us right with God. Getting right with God is what justification accomplishes, and that is God's free gift to us. Good works flow from true faith. In other words, when we get right with God, we start doing good things. Does Bishop Curry understand this, is this what he is saying?

He argues for racial reconciliation. Who opposes that? But if racial reconciliation is little more than bashing white privilege, then it will fail. 98% percent of all the bills in TEC are paid for by whites -- increasingly by late middle-aged white women who make up two-thirds of the Church. Curry needs to be careful who he calls racist. Anti-racism training for generations of aging Episcopalians is nothing short of making a group of people feel guilty for things they have never said or done. It might also be a case of bullying on a mass scale.

Bishop Curry wants to have "both supporters and opponents of same-sex marriage" at the table. Curry said he wants to preside over a welcoming church open to all people -- including gay couples. This is not going to happen. In fact, nearly all of those who reject same-sex marriage have left TEC for the Anglican Church in North America, the Roman Catholic Church by way of the Ordinariate, or have gone directly to Rome.

Same sex marriage is totally off the table for orthodox Episcopalians. Only a handful of dioceses have said they would not ordain or marry gay couples. These dioceses include Albany, Springfield, North Dakota, Northern Indiana and Central Florida, though the latter is conflicted over the issue.

No clergy opposed to same-sex marriage will be compelled to act against his or her conscience by performing one, so we are told. "We respect conscience, just as we respect and honor gays and lesbians who wish to receive the holy sacrament of matrimony," Curry said. "That's a church that's working to be, as Jesus said, quoting the prophets, 'a house of prayer for all people.' We're making room for all."

We heard that mantra from another Presiding Bishop, Frank Griswold, who opined in Philadelphia, "My door is open to all". It was a lie, of course. He spent most of his ecclesiological capital pushing pansexuality onto the communion and failed.

We also saw what happened to opponents of women's ordination. In time, those who opposed WO were drummed out of the church; the same will happen, in time, with those who refuse to marry gays. Tell that to all the dioceses in serious litigation with the Episcopal Church over who owns church property. Will he stop the litigation now that he is Presiding Bishop? To date, he has not done so.

Furthermore, Bishop Curry had no option but to enforce General Convention resolutions on same sex marriage canons under pressure from the Integrity organization and the ultra-liberal revisionist wing of his bishops. This happened just as women's ordination was ultimately forced on the whole church, alienating bishops like John-David Schofield, Jack Iker and Keith Ackerman.

It all came to a head in July of 2018, when the Episcopal Church at its 79th General Convention overwhelmingly passed Resolution B012 mandating homosexual marriage. It was the final straw for the Bishop of Albany, the Rt. Rev. William Love. He demurred. As a result, Presiding Bishop Curry temporarily restricted part of the bishop's ministry. The restriction applied both to the Episcopal Church's formal Title IV disciplinary process and to any action "that has or may have the effect of penalizing in any way any member of the clergy or laity or worshipping congregation of his diocese for their participation in the arrangements for or participation in a same-sex marriage in his diocese or elsewhere."

Curry also said Love's conduct surrounding the issue "may constitute a canonical offense," namely for violating his ordination vows and for conduct unbecoming a member of the clergy. Unbowed, Love said he would fight the charges in an ecclesiastical court.

Gracious conversation is at best a myth, at worst a lie. That ship sailed a long time ago. The ACNA was birthed out of the heresies of TEC and no one is going back. No one.

Is the Jesus Movement Christian?

Is the Jesus Movement really Christian? In truth, the Jesus Movement depersonalizes Jesus. He is no longer the Jesus of history who is the Christ of faith, he is an impersonal "movement" who can be manipulated to meet our needs not to succumb to Curry's demands.

The much-ballyhooed Covenant designed to find middle ground over sexuality issues came to nothing. The Covenant, said Dr. Rowan Williams, was about being accountable to each other in the Communion. As in any family, what we do affects those with whom we are in a relationship. The Covenant is about thinking through those relationships, and what the consequences are of whatever we choose to do in our own particular bit of the Communion's life.

There is little belief that under Presiding Bishop Michael Curry that the Covenant will go anywhere. He is focusing his call on the Jesus Movement. To all intents and purposes, the Covenant died under Jefferts Schori.

Curry and other bishops had a less than true biblical understanding of Jesus. They called him Jesus of Nazareth and do not refer to him the way the post-resurrection Bible does. In Acts after Pentecost, Peter calls him Lord Jesus. In his sermon in Acts 2:22, Peter says, "Jesus the Nazarene was a man commended to you by God by the miracles and portents and signs that God worked through him when he was among you." After Peter describes the resurrection and supports this with scripture, Peter says, "For this reason the whole House of Israel can be certain that the Lord and Christ whom God has made is this Jesus whom you crucified."

After that, Christians connected the historical name of Jesus with the name Christ, Messiah in Hebrew and Lord of the universe. Paul calls him Jesus Christ, Lord Jesus Christ and Christ Jesus. The point is that Jesus of Nazareth is the promised Christ, the expected Messiah and so the faithful call him Jesus Christ.

But Michael Curry, Shannon Johnston, the Bishop of Virginia and others do not. This is their 'Jesus Movement' remembering Jesus of Nazareth and his social vision.

That is who the Episcopal House of Bishops wants us to remember. Not the resurrected, glorified Christ who tells us, "I am the Alpha and Omega, the first and the last, the beginning and the end."

To strip Jesus of his role as the Christ of God, to ignore that he is the Lord of the Universe and to deny that without him nothing was made, is beyond the pale. It is truly a "game changer" as Michael Curry is fond of saying. If his game changer goes through, then it is surely a time to worry. It is a time to confront the leadership within the Episcopal Church with their taking away Christ, hiding his sacrificial death, ignoring the resurrection, and deciding the people in the Episcopal Church are so theologically illiterate that they won't even notice.

The Jesus Movement is the culmination and fulfillment of the heretical Bishop James Albert Pike's theology that began in the 1960s.

Curry knows the church is dying. He needs to know he has no power without the next generation; screaming about the Jesus Movement will not fill emptying pews. It's not just about dialogue. It's called repenting for losing sight of the Gospel and not even bothering to look for it.

If there is another generation of Christians, they will have to rediscover what and who Jesus is, that He is Lord of history and Lord of our lives and they will worship Christ as did the Apostle Thomas when he cried out, "My Lord and my God!"

Now we have 'Kermit the Frog' and 'Don't Worry be Happy' and 'Just Believe', along with some digs at the ACNA.

We need a Reformation where the Episcopal Bishops, and particularly the Presiding Bishop, cease and desist from grabbing popular imaginative creations from our culture and claim that this is following Jesus.

One young person put it well when he said, "This is all that 1960s stuff we are trying to avoid."

Perhaps Curry knows that. Preaching anti-racism to white people who are not racist and pressing the subtext of White Privilege will not win back generations of white (or black) Americans. This "propaganda" is just a disingenuous effort to keep the money coming from those who were part of the 1960s. Hoping that popular imagery from their youth will keep their checkbooks open is short term thinking, but long-term loss.

Curry as the "love" Bishop

On May 19, 2018, two royal love birds, Prince Harry and Meghan Markle were married in St George's Chapel at Windsor Castle in the

United Kingdom. The preacher was Michael Curry, The Episcopal Church's Presiding Bishop. He came at the invitation of the Archbishop of Canterbury, Justin Welby.

In his sermon, Curry talked endlessly of love and hope and his words and manner caught the world's attention. He became an instant celebrity and was dutifully nicknamed the "love bishop."

What he preached, examined in the hard light of day, and in hindsight, was not overflowing with biblical insight or expository preaching.

As Anglican Bishop Gavin Ashenden observed, "it can be very appealing. It reaches out to where people are hurting and it encourages them. It reaches out to where they are longing for good change, and it promises them that change can come." What he offered, however, was 'Christianity-lite'. The opposite was 'Christianity-max'.

Curry spoke continuously of love and hope. But the sermon had three serious flaws. He didn't define love; he never delivered on the hope and it isn't what Jesus preached.

Michael Curry did not elucidate a Christian view of cupid and eros. He simply accepted cupid and eros and celebrated how wonderful they were.

Even an amateur theologian might reply to him; "wrong gods, Bishop Curry."

And then he moved into the political as all progressives do.

And this is the hope that always lets us down. It is the Hebrew prophets who give fire and articulation to this hope, says Ashenden. "They see God as delivering political and personal transformation at the end of time; only then will the lion lie down with the lamb; only then will the tears be wiped away from our eyes, and by God himself, not by the army of emoting counsellors of the progressive utopia."

Curry told the world that Harry and Meghan loved each other so much that we would see the 'end of poverty.' Of course, this was conditional on everyone loving each other as much as Meghan and

Harry; and conditional on no one getting jealous or falling out of love or getting bored with each other. But he didn't point that out.

Although that is, of course, what happens to almost everyone. And this falling out of love, this passing beyond the gravitational pull of romance and eros happens to all lovers, at some point.

The Gospel according to Hollywood (for that is what it is) directs that you jettison your original love, once they no longer give you what you need, and replace them with another. Cupid is a demanding god happy to sacrifice human beings to the feelings of narcissistic eroticized amorousness he engenders.

Since the condition is not and cannot be kept, Curry misled the people.

Misleading the people in God's name is not the calling of a Christian bishop, even if, as Ed Miliband a British politician and former leader of the Labour Party tweeted, "this bishop almost makes me believe in God.' Yes, almost. But he didn't make Milliband believe in God. And if he had, it would not anyway have been the Holy God of Israel and the prophets and of His Son Jesus Christ. It would have been the god of the romanticized and eroticized self; a lesser god. A counterfeit god.

It was a *pièce de résistance* example of the vacuous variety of faith which Richard Niebuhr so forensically described as consisting of "A God without wrath who brought men without sin into a Kingdom without judgment through the ministrations of a Christ without a Cross."

Curry promised, but he failed to deliver.

"When love is the way — unselfish, sacrificial, redemptive, when love is the way. Then no child would go to bed hungry in this world ever again. When love is the way. We will let justice roll down like a mighty stream and righteousness like an ever-flowing brook. When love is the way poverty will become history. When love is the way the earth will become a sanctuary."

But the place where 'max' differs from Curry's lite is at the crossroads of repentance. The god that Curry preached was a god who gives romance and erotic love and neighborly generosity without any conditions attached.

But Jesus said there were conditions attached. And they were the surrender of the ego, the plucking out of eyes that offended, the cutting off of hands that grasped in the wrong direction; it was conditional on repentance.,

Bishop Curry told an 'untruth' in fact, and a most serious distortion of the teaching of Jesus, who is the Way, the Truth and the Life. Untruth does not serve Him.

Only when the ego is surrendered; only when romance and eros are dethroned; only when a person has reached the end of their natural tether, can the Lord God be invited in, and the process of personal transformation begin.

If enough people turn in repentance to Jesus, we might see improved societies. We did, following the Wesleyan revival. We did, following the Tractarian revival. But Bishop Curry did not choose to add the condition 'if enough persons turn to Jesus.'

Of course, as the Daily Mail and other media outlets trumpeted, Bishop Curry is a famous advocate for homosexuality and transgenderism. Of course, he is, because if there is no requirement for repentance, then the neo-Marxist preference for those at the bottom of power structures mean that irrespective of the sexual ethics of the New Testament, homosexual love and gender dysphoria need special promotion and protection.

But the Marxist power ethic that favors minorities is not found in the mouth of Jesus. In the mouth of Jesus, we find a call for repentance and an aiming to the highest ethics of sexual morality.

By depriving the world audience of the promise that lies at the heart of God's invitation to turn, Bishop Curry deprived them of the very transformation he was selling them.

Yes, Bishop Curry, as St. John wrote, God is love. But unlike Curry, St John defines Love and shows us that it is a longing and meeting of longing that travels the way of the cross, the way of renunciation.

But if you want to be popular, don't invite the people to renunciation. And Bishop Curry didn't. Jesus did.

There are two kinds of Anglicanism practiced in the world today. One that contains the cross and repentance and touches and transforms sexual desire, and one that doesn't. People who don't intend to change their ways prefer the one that doesn't. That was the one that Bishop Curry offered them. It will change nothing; because it wasn't Christianity. It was 'Christianity-lite'.

Curry's Book Crazy Christians

In his book, Curry talks about transforming the Lord. He actually said, "Transform the world."

What he means though is to transform the Lord and Savior of the Universe Jesus Christ. Transform him from our kind and merciful Savior to a critical one.

"You are my biggest headache," Curry writes in his book that God says this to us. Is this little more than psychological abuse?

Transform the Lord from one who has sexual standards to one who allows, well, anything.

"The change in sexual morality is a game changer!" he cries.

Transform the Lord from the one who says, "If you want to build a tower, count the costs" Luke 14: 28 to one who tells us to be risky and dangerous.

People hear that Christ is no longer honored. We are following the teachings of Jesus. Really? Did Jesus tell us to sue hundreds of priests and their parishes to get their wealth and buildings? Jesus tells us that faith is like a fictional magician walking over Niagara Falls on a tightrope?

In his address to the 77th General Convention of the Episcopal Church in Indianapolis in July, 2012, Curry said this;

> We need some Christians who are as crazy as the Lord. Crazy enough to love like Jesus, to give like Jesus, to forgive like Jesus, to do justice, love mercy, walk humbly with God— like Jesus. Crazy enough to dare to change the world from the nightmare it often is into something close to the dream that God dreams for it. And for those who would follow him, those who would be his disciples, for those who would live as and be the people of the Way? It might come as a shock, but they are called to craziness.

Curry exclaims in his book, "We are crazy Christians!"

Curry develops a shame-based theology. "God didn't create me because God needs me. In fact, if the truth be told, I'm one of God's biggest headaches. And I'll let you in on a secret—you're the other one."

Does writing get more hateful than this? Exactly what does it mean to be God's biggest headache? The Christian gospel is that we are all sinners to be redeemed by Jesus Christ. We Christians are not a headache to God.

So, in the Jesus Movement Curry calls us God's biggest headache, He tells us it is not easy being green, but don't worry, be happy.

Jesus Christ is not part of Presiding Bishop Michael Curry's Jesus Movement. And as often as Curry yells this phrase, no one is picking up on it and following Curry. Nor will they get into his imaginary wheelbarrow being pushed across Niagara Falls in the hope that no one falls. Because if they do, they might fall into the arms, not of the savior of the world, but into the arms of the Evil One where no hope or Jesus is to be found.

TEC'S FUTURE:
The Numbers Don't Lie

On any reckoning the future of The Episcopal Church looks bleak. Within two generations, most of the Church will be gone. There will be hold out parishes like Trinity Wall Street, the richest church in the world, and a number of large Texas parishes. But the smaller parishes will die, merge and then be sold off to start up evangelical churches, boutiques and emergent Muslim groups. Whole dioceses will be forced to juncture.

There are no new young generations coming forward in significant numbers to fill either the pews or pulpits.

Aging Episcopalians are slowly filling church yard columbarium's even as aging, retired priests temporarily fill pulpits.

An employment survey by The Church Pension Group in 2018 revealed a new landscape. Their results demonstrated a clear difference in models of employment by geography and gender, and a decline in the "old model" of full-time employment at a single Episcopal entity until retirement.

The survey produced 11 profiles of priests, ranging from those in traditional full-time employment, through various forms of part-time, bi-vocational, and supply, to those with no work.

A slim majority of active-age respondents (52%) were still within the traditional model:

Compared to those serving part-time at a single parish, the proportions of men to women serving full-time are almost exactly reversed: full-time male 62%, female 38%; part-time male 31%, female 69%.

Women also made up a large majority of the supply category (73%), and a significant majority of those in non-stipendiary positions (57%).

While priests reporting no employment made up only 2% of the survey sample, women were again over-represented in the results (65% female to 35% male).

Plenty of priests outside of the "norm" wish they were within it.

The CPG reported the following takeaways:

'Women perceive that they are less likely to get "traditional" positions'.

'Parishes can't afford a full-time priest, but still have expectations for full-time ministry'.

'It's not just the parishes that are financially stressed' [but also clergy].

'Full-time rectorships are few and hard to come by."

'A single career break has long-lasting consequences.'

'The "norm" is no longer the "norm"'.

The deeper issue is the message coming from pulpits. The "gospel" of homosexual inclusion and diversity have not now nor ever filled parishes and nor have they brought younger generations into the pews.

History will show that the seminaries created a generation of theologically vacuous bishops; the bishops employed priests of a like-minded nature, and the priests sold pansexual platitudes and easy-believism from the pulpits. One reporter noted that while other mainline denominations are declining because they lack a distinctive brand, The Episcopal Church still has two small but continuous pipelines of new members: post-Evangelicals and liberal Catholics. That may be true, but they will not be large enough to save The Episcopal Church.

In the words of the prophet Hosea; The Episcopal Church has sown to the wind and it has reaped the whirlwind and for that it has no one to blame but itself. The spiritual stalks of grain have withered and produced nothing to eat. The people look up and are not fed.

As Jesus himself observed; "When he saw the crowds, he had compassion on them, because they were harassed and helpless, like sheep without a shepherd." Episcopal Church shepherds gutted the churches by failing to preach a clear and undiluted gospel. This has resulted in spiritual death with the life of Christ and the person of the Holy Spirit evaporating from the churches never more to return. The glory of God has departed forever from the Episcopal Church. Ichabod.

END

Photo Credits

Page 1 – Los Angeles Times, August 6, 1966, James A. Pike, Episcopal Bishop of California at San Francisco, Image, Wikipedia, 9/29/2019 {https://en.wikipedia.org/wiki/File:James_a_pike.jpg} CC BY-SA 2.5

Page 13 – RW Holmen, November 14, 2013, Dr. Louie Crew and Ernest Clay, Image, The blog of RW Holmen, 9/29/2019 {http://www.theliberalspirit.com/cast-of-characters-countdown-louie-clay-crew/} CC BY-SA 3.0

Page 25 – Sheryl A. Kujawa, 2016, Bishop Edmund Browning, Image, The Episcopal Church, New York, NY, 9/29/2019 {https://www.episcopalchurch.org/library/article/there-will-be-no-outcasts-official-obituary-edmond-lee-browning } CC BY-SA 3.0

Page 39 – Randy OHC, December 10, 2007, Bishop Frank Griswold, Image, Wikipedia, 9/29/2019 {https://en.wikipedia.org/wiki/Frank_Griswold#/media/File:2007FrankGriswold-flickr-RandyOHC.jpg} CC BY-SA 2.0

Page 77 – Tom McFeely, October 21, 2008, Bishop Katharine Jefferts Schori, Image, National Catholic Register, 9/29/2019 {http://www.ncregister.com/blog/tom-Mcfeely/those_inclusive_episcopalians}

Page 113 – December 9, 2015, Bishop Michael Curry, Image, The Living Church, Milwaukee, WI 9/29/2019 {https://livingchurch.org/2015/12/09/presiding-bishop-clears-surgery}

David W. Virtue has been writing about Anglican issues for more than 30 years. He has been a pioneer in writing Anglican news from an orthodox perspective. He has received theological training in the UK, US and Canada and brings a wealth of theological insight into reporting the news for Anglicans globally. VIRTUEONLINE is the most widely read orthodox Anglican Online News Service, which annually reaches over 4 million readers in 170 countries.